QUIET
Influence

Berrett-Koehler Publishers, Inc.
235 Montgomery Street, Suite 650
San Francisco, CA 94104-2916
Tel: (415) 288-0260 Fax: (415) 362-2512 www.bkconnection.com

Ordering Information

Quantity sales. Special discounts are available on quantity purchases by corporations, associations, and others. For details, contact the "Special Sales Department" at the Berrett-Koehler address above.

Individual sales. Berrett-Koehler publications are available through most bookstores. They can also be ordered directly from Berrett-Koehler:
Tel: (800) 929-2929; Fax: (802) 864-7626; www.bkconnection.com

Orders for college textbook/course adoption use. Please contact Berrett-Koehler:
Tel: (800) 929-2929; Fax: (802) 864-7626.

Orders by U.S. trade bookstores and wholesalers. Please contact Ingram Publisher Services, Tel: (800) 509-4887; Fax: (800) 838-1149; E-mail: customer.service@ ingrampublisherservices.com; or visit www.ingrampublisherservices.com/Ordering for details about electronic ordering.

Berrett-Koehler and the BK logo are registered trademarks of Berrett-Koehler Publishers, Inc.

Printed in the United States of America

Berrett-Koehler books are printed on long-lasting acid-free paper. When it is available, we choose paper that has been manufactured by environmentally responsible processes. These may include using trees grown in sustainable forests, incorporating recycled paper, minimizing chlorine in bleaching, or recycling the energy produced at the paper mill.

Library of Congress Cataloging-in-Publication Data

Kahnweiler, Jennifer B.
    Quiet influence : the introvert's guide to making a difference / Jennifer B.
    Kahnweiler, PhD. -- First Edition.
      pages cm
    Includes bibliographical references and index.
    ISBN 978-1-60994-562-6 (pbk.)
    1. Interpersonal communication. 2. Introverts. I. Title.
    HM1166.K34 2013
    155.2'32--dc23
                                         2012049169

First Edition
18 17 16 15 14 13   10 9 8 7 6 5 4 3 2 1

Project management and interior design by Dovetail Publishing Services
Cover design and production by PermaStudio

QUIET
Influence

The Introvert's Guide to Making a Difference

Jennifer B. Kahnweiler, PhD

BK

Berrett–Koehler Publishers, Inc.
San Francisco
a BK Life book

*To Bill, who has quietly influenced me
to love him . . . then and now.*

Contents

Preface

"In every performance review, I'm told I need to speak up more. That I need to spend less time in my office with my door closed. My boss says I have to 'sell' my ideas with more enthusiasm. My co-workers say that I need to be more of a 'team player' and less of a 'report generator.' Believe me, I've tried. It seems that when I try to develop those skills, though, I'm just acting like someone else. I feel as if I have less of an impact rather than more. How can I be me and still make a difference?"

Sari sighed and shrugged her shoulders with more than a hint of frustration as she posed the question to me during a workshop I was leading at her company. I've been asked a similar question many times, and I always feel a sense of sorrow in answering. The reality is that introverts are indeed continually asked to adapt to an extrovert-centric workplace that rewards being out there and on stage. Organizational cultures support those who talk about their accomplishments, who spend more time out and about networking instead of alone deep in thought, and who make sure they are the first to get their ideas heard.

If you are an introvert, you probably feel as perplexed and underappreciated as Sari. Know that you are not alone and that there is a solution—one that not only honors who you are but also dramatically and immediately ramps up your ability to make a difference at work. *Quiet Influence* gives you that solution and shows that it resides precisely in the place where you are most comfortable: deep inside yourself.

This book is not about how introverts need to adapt to an outgoing, extroverted world. Instead, it's about learning from the Quiet Influencers among us who are making just as much, if not more, of a difference than their extroverted colleagues.

It's just that they are going about it in such a, well . . . quiet way that few seem to notice them. So many books about influence miss the mark, extolling a more extroverted approach that involves winning people over by talking things up, presenting great arguments and quickly and aggressively convincing others to do what they want them to do.

Over my years of working with introverted professionals and studying the process of influence, *I have become convinced that introverts can be highly effective influencers when they stop trying to act like extroverts and instead make the most of their natural, quiet strengths.*

Because you've probably tried the extroverted methods, why not take a walk on the quiet side? You can become a more effective influencer when you tap into your natural strengths, and in the pages that follow I'm going to show you how. You'll recognize your strengths and learn ways to enhance and magnify them. You will deepen your understanding of how introverts like you succeed at influence. If you are open to building on your natural strengths through conscious practice, you will perfect core skills, develop heightened sensibilities, and bump up your confidence to influence all kinds of people and situations. As a result, you will greatly enhance your influencing success rate by embracing an alternative to traditionally western Type A approaches to interactions.

Perhaps you land more on the extroverted side of the line as someone energized by people and the outside world. Why not take a walk on the quiet side? Through this book, you will deepen your understanding of how introverts succeed at influence. You will find that learning from introverts offers an enlightening opportunity to balance out your own (likely louder) ways of influencing. If you are open to experimenting with a different side of yourself, you will greatly enhance your own influencing portfolio so that you can have a bigger impact in a wider variety of situations. You'll get noticed precisely because you are trying something new.

Introduction

Why Quiet Influence, Why Now?

Do you work in a company? How about in a nonprofit that competes for funding?

Do you work in a government agency with contractors?

Are you an entrepreneur or freelancer who sells products or services?

Are you in technology, engineering, or science?

Do you work in sales, marketing, project management, teaching, medicine, the law, human resources, or administration?

The truth is that everyone in a professional role needs to influence others. From Seoul to Seattle, today's competitive workplace demands that you influence a variety of situations and people, not once in a while but multiple times a day. Although influence is sometimes about really big issues and opportunities, it is also about nudging change along one small step at a time.

Noted researchers such as Jay Conger ("The Necessary Art of Persuasion") have found that selling ideas and getting people on board is a process, not an event.[1] Influence is not about forcing people to come to see things your way but about learning from

1

others and negotiating a shared solution. This approach is well suited to the introvert temperament. It involves patience, planning, and perseverance. If we all think that the only way to get things done is to shout louder and louder and take up more center-stage space, we'll miss the opportunities to listen, learn, and respond thoughtfully.

It may be that our society is starting to get this message. Extroverts are slowly (very slowly, some argue) realizing that we stand to lose the wisdom and contributions of more than half of the population if we don't listen to the introverts in our world. Since the 2009 publication of my last book, *The Introverted Leader: Building on Your Quiet Strength* (the first book about introverted leaders), a firestorm of other books (including Susan Cain's 2012 *New York Times* bestseller *Quiet*), articles and social media have crusaded for the cause of introverts. I have been gratified to hear the buzz of such conversations everywhere.

Moreover, even though they will never really experience how an introvert truly feels, extroverts are starting to get the differences on a personal level. They push their pens in my hand to sign a copies of *The Introverted Leader* for their sons, spouses, and siblings, who they never quite understood. Hope for a broader change springs from such a personal connection.

Perhaps the strongest driver for Quiet Influence, however, is how it can contribute to success in today's shifting workplace. These four trends indicate that the time for Quiet Influence is now:

1. Flattened organizations and complex vendor, supplier, and customer interactions mean that you must, no matter what your position or personality type, be effective at getting your ideas heard. Gone are the days when you can rely on a boss or your boss's boss to make your case for you. You have to establish critical relationships and communicate key messages yourself.

2. Going global means that you need to find multiple ways to influence an increasingly diverse set of colleagues and customers.

For example, your more reflective, low-key influencing approach will be much more effective with your colleagues in Asia than a traditional extroverted one. You can use your Quiet Influence skills to make a difference with those in cultures that value a quieter approach.

3. The virtual world is evolving and ever present. In today's society, it's highly unlikely that you can influence a broad group of people without using digital media in purposeful ways. Introverts, as particularly thoughtful users of social media, may well be ahead of the game. They have been drawn to social media because it lets them use their strengths and better manage their communication. You and other Quiet Influencers who have already invested in learning and using social media are poised to effect tomorrow's change more quickly than influencers who have ignored these technologies.

4. Heightened competition for business and jobs means that companies are seeking suppliers and employees who bring fresh, innovative approaches. The truth is, extrovert-centric self-promotion and loud persuasion are passé. Today, you will stand out from the crowd if you have a knack for building up others and are committed to listening instead of talking.

Because Quiet Influence is already what you do naturally, these trends offer you the impetus to enhance those skills. Your time has come. This book is written to help you and millions of other introverts recognize, develop, and highlight your innate influencing strengths. Together, you make up about 50 percent of the world's population, and you can make a big difference in organizations and communities around the world. I encourage you to applaud the success of your strengths and practice making a difference without making a lot of noise.

I believe that as these trends intensify, the tide will turn and extroverts will want to learn Quiet Influencing strengths from the introverts they know. Many extroverts recognize that they are more effective, flexible, adaptable influencers when their influencing toolbox includes a wider variety of approaches.

I'll admit it: I am one such extrovert. I needed to practice how to make a difference without making a lot of noise. For much of my professional life, I went along with the ill-founded belief that the Type A approach, with its emphasis on talking and finding center stage, delivered results. I am a speaker, executive coach, and author whose job it is to influence people to try new approaches in their lives. Of course, I thought, that means being "out there" and being "on." I moved very fast, did a lot of winging it, and often found a way to attract attention. As I progressed in my career, I embodied the stereotype of the loud, assertive New Yorker I was.

Yet I grew up quietly watching people. My dad, Alvin Boretz, was a TV and film screenwriter, and many of our dinner conversations were about people, their motivations and behavior. Because Dad's work depended on picking up the nuances of dialogue, the meanings of conversations were of endless interest to our family. It was not unusual to see my extroverted family of four sitting quietly in Cairo's, our local Italian restaurant, listening to simultaneous conversations around us. On the way home, we would share dialogues we overheard and wonder aloud about the lives and relationships of our fellow diners. The introverts offered few verbal clues, so we had a field day guessing what could have been going on in their lives. Those quieter, low-key families, so different from ours, were especially intriguing to me. What was going on with them?

I embarked on my career and continued to be an observer of introverts. I was still people watching, and the people who continued to intrigue me were the introverts—those people who sometimes struggled in leadership positions even though they had all the power they needed deep inside. I wrote *The Introverted Leader: Building on Your Quiet Strength* to give these talented people a guide for being in charge while being themselves.

During the research for that book and in countless interactions since its publication, I have found myself increasingly drawn to the stories and experiences of introverts. The more I speak with, listen to, coach, and write about introverts, the more I appreciate their sensibility. I have realized that the quiet language of the introvert is refreshingly different from my natural outgoing persona, and I recognize that I can incorporate introverted traits and behaviors in order to have a greater impact. For instance, instead of rushing on to that conference call at the last minute, I can spend some quiet time sitting on my deck watching the trees and reflecting on my purpose for the day. Or in lieu of randomly posting something on Facebook, I can think of the other tasks that await me. Or in working through a sticky relationship, I can write out my thoughts to gain clarity on where I stand.

All in all, I recognize that a powerful shift occurs in me when I flow into the less prominent side of my personality. When I choose to embrace my internal energy, I gain deeper insights, delve into my creativity, and become more centered. Jungian psychologists would say that I am releasing a potent force by tapping into the less dominant side of my temperament. I simply see that I have been influenced by the introverts I set out to influence.

Inspired by the Quiet Influencers I have met and the effect they had on me, I turned my attention to the question of *how* these successful introverts make a difference. How exactly do they challenge the status quo, provoke new ways of thinking, or inspire others to move forward? What inner strengths do they call upon to effect change? What steps do they take to influence others?

In my professional life, I have interacted with thousands of people who deepened my knowledge of the introvert experience and gave me ideas about how to answer these questions. Class discussions, questions after speeches, and problems that surfaced in coaching sessions have all contributed to my understanding and perspective. In my role as an author and journalist, I met a wide range of introverts and have written and been interviewed for a number of articles on the topic of introverts in the workplace for publications such as *Forbes, Bloomberg Business Week,* and the *Wall Street Journal.* Through hallway conversations, follow-up emails, and blog comments, I have gained an even deeper understanding about how introverts experience their world and the ways in which they use their natural strengths to get through to people in powerful ways.

I have also been fortunate to be plugged into a vibrant community of Quiet Influencers. I specifically asked these professionals from a wide range of fields and organizations about their approach to influence. They often provided written responses, and I followed up with phone interviews to enhance my understanding. In their characteristically humble way, they shared about the myriad ways in which they make a difference with other people and organizations. As privacy-valuing introverts, several of these Quiet Influencers asked that their names not be used. In those cases, I have replaced their name with a first-name-only pseudonym. Many others agreed that I could use their names, and I have included those in the text.

I have done my best to capture the stories that motivated me as I sought to answer my driving question: *how do they make an impact by building on their natural, quiet strengths?* I then distilled their answers into the six strengths you will read about in the chapters ahead. In these strengths, I hope you find your own unique expression of Quiet Influence.

Chapter 1

Stop Trying to Act Like an Extrovert

"Lower your voice and strengthen your argument."

Barbara McAfee, Author and Singer

Did you know that . . .

The best ideas often emerge in the depths of solitude?

Writing a persuasive email may move a project along faster than a standard conversation?

Listening for what is not said is more important than listening for what is?

Quiet Influencers—those people who make things happen without in-your-face techniques—learned these lessons through experience. Like ripples in a pond they deliver a big impact without making a loud fuss. When introverts need to be influencers, they focus on careful thought and depth. There isn't much fanfare or much noise. In their quiet, humble way, introverted influencers make sure that the people they are hoping to impact get the message. Yet they are frequently overlooked and underestimated by organizations and colleagues who buy into the idea that talking reigns supreme.

7

If you are an introvert, chances are that you've tried to influence others by mirroring your more outgoing colleagues. My guess is that such an approach isn't working for you: it's exhausting, unsustainable, and ultimately ineffective. Contrary to what most books on influence will tell you, the answer isn't about becoming the extrovert you aren't. *I believe, however, that you will become a more effective influencer when you stop trying to act like an extrovert and instead make the most of your natural, quiet strengths.* By sharing specific stories and tips from successful Quiet Influencers, this book will show you how to identify, magnify, and apply those natural strengths so that you can make a big difference without making a lot of noise. You will discover how you can acknowledge your internal energy, tap into its wisdom, and thoughtfully engage with the outside world.

The Roadblocks to Quiet Influence

Certainly, the louder extroverted approach dominates the workplace today. That approach, which negates the natural tendencies of more than half of the population, sets up roadblocks to Quiet Influence. Do any of these roadblocks resonate with you?

1. Focus on Teams

Back in the 1980s, corporations jumped on the teams-produce-results bandwagon, and the group approach proliferated, bringing us today's reality: professional work most often necessitates teamwork. Your supervisor may be called your "team leader," and your work group is likely called a "team." Our workstations are arranged so that we can sit with our teams, we do most of our work in "team meetings," we generate ideas through brainstorming, we strive to meet team objectives, and most people are not hired until they have interviewed with all members of the team. For introverts, this team-heavy approach presents a problem. Not only does being intertwined with others deplete their reserves of people energy, it also takes them away from the physical and intellectual space, where they do their best thinking. If you are an introvert, you know that need to be alone to reflect and create. There is so much pressure that introverts talk about escaping to "bathroom solitude." In fact, in a survey I conducted of one hundred introverts, four out of five said they "suffered from people exhaustion."[2] With this pressure to be engaged with people all day, Quiet Influencers have a hard time finding the quiet time and preparation to hatch their plans.

2. The Need to Talk about Accomplishments and Ideas

In most organizations, sharing your accomplishments contributes to your personal "brand." People come to know you and appreciate the value you offer because you've talked about yourself and what you've done. The problem is that those folks who don't "brag on themselves" (i.e., most introverts) often find themselves unwittingly out of the loop. If they don't have a boss who seeks their input, showcases their talent, and enhances their visibility, they are often left behind. Today's corporate cultures do not reward humility. This characteristic restraint often results in being overlooked. Introverts have great ideas that go unheard. In group settings, they may show up with smart solutions, yet can't seem to find an opening in which to share them. Even in one-on-one conversations—especially with extroverts—they have trouble interjecting their ideas and being heard. Because these quiet people haven't talked themselves up, they tend to fly under the radar, and few extroverted colleagues think to draw them out to share their ideas. The introvert therefore finds it difficult to get people's attention and use that attention to influence situations.

3. The Pressure to Act Extroverted

Many Asian cultures deeply value the ability to not show much emotion. Western workplaces, however, barely tolerate expressionless faces or quiet people. It seems that to fit in, you have to be animated and verbal. Not your style? Too bad. To succeed, you have to fake it.

Oliver Goldsmith, the 18th-century Irish writer, described a character by saying, "On the stage he was natural, simple, and affecting. 'Twas only when he was off, he was acting." Introverts often express a similar feeling. They "act the part" of being happy, sociable, and expressive even when they are feeling quite different. Susan Cain, the author of *Quiet: The Power of Introverts in a World that Can't Stop Talking*, refers to this pressure as living up to the "Extrovert Ideal."[3] One Quiet Influencer describes small talk at business events as the sounds of "competitive egos." When she joins in she feels inauthentic.

Yet challenging the status quo and inspiring others to move forward takes a willingness to show your real self to others. Introverts find their influencing efforts impeded when others sense they are difficult to read and when they themselves are exhausted by the pressure to be "on."

4. Making Quick Decisions

From answering a question in a meeting to responding to an overnight email from a customer, today's environment pressures people to make quick decisions. Many workplaces value instant responses over well-thought-out ones that take a little longer. The speed of technology and an increasingly competitive global climate have revved up the pace of work. The time to ponder a sticky problem from various angles has evaporated. The "what if" questions and the chance to go back to gather more data before deciding are gone. The people we are trying to sell our ideas and products to want results now.

Unfortunately, introverts once again get the short end of the stick. They are frustrated when they are unable to slow down the decision-making process. They are not able to take the needed time to process decisions in their head and do the necessary preparation to yield the best results. Others then often label them as "slow" and behind the curve, and they find it difficult to be treated with the respect they deserve. While they are pondering decisions and analyzing the situation, they often fail to pick up the cues that they are about to be left behind. Their "delay" often costs them the opportunities to influence the decision.

5. Lowered Privacy Boundaries

Similar to unwanted probing at social events, social media sites like Facebook pile on the pressure for us to open up our inner selves to the outer world. The lower privacy boundaries create an uncomfortable climate for introverts, who like to get to know someone before baring their soul. They contend with the notion of TMI (too much information) on a daily basis.

Savvy introverts know they need to build relationships to influence others. They simply want to get to know people slowly instead of jumping right to the personal stuff. The pressure to share and connect every day at an accelerated pace stresses them out, depletes their energy, and challenges the very relationships they are seeking to build on their own terms.

6. Being Talked Over

Of all the roadblocks to Quiet Influence, being talked over is the one that seems to frustrate introverts the most. In the talkative climate of Western society, interruptions abound. If an introvert speaks quietly or takes a pause, others jump in and steal the stage. Even if an introvert is speaking at a normal volume, eloquently expressing an idea he or she has fully developed before offering it, extroverts are likely to interrupt. To the extrovert who tends to think out loud, the interruption is merely a way of building off of the introvert's good idea. To the introvert, the interruption is like a blanket that silences his or her voice. Introverts' ideas cease to be explored by the group, and they tend to surrender to the opinions of the loudest person in the room. The result: introverts are demotivated and less inclined to float new ideas.

Moreover, introverts feel pressure to participate in the interruption game. Many introverts from Asia comment that they hear two competing voices in their head: their parents saying "be polite" and their boss telling them they need to "speak up" and interject their comments in meetings. This instruction creates a deep conflict for introverts who prefer to marinate their thoughts, taking advantage of a pause in the conversation not to speak, but to think. Not only do they face the frustration of being talked over, but they are encouraged to impose a style on others in a way that fights with their very nature.

If these roadblocks sound familiar to you and invoke feelings of frustration, know you are not alone. You are simply an introvert stuck in an extrovert-centric world. Instead of trying to avoid these roadblocks on the extrovert highway, take a more direct, efficient, and enjoyable route. Embrace what you do naturally and see greater results. Other introverts have done it: they are out there delivering the next possible cure for cancer, the answer to global warming, and the fix for education. You can do it too.

Characteristics that Shape Introverts

Hopefully you're getting the message that you don't have to be an extrovert to be a great influencer. You can succeed by embracing your introverted nature. But what does the term introvert really mean? It's a term many people throw around these days but few people really understand.

Let's start with a fundamental question: When you need to recharge, do you tend to want to be alone in a quiet place? If you answered yes, you're likely an introvert.

Technically speaking, *introversion* and *extroversion* are terms that refer to personality traits and are about sources of stimulation and energy. Although extroverts recharge by being with people and participating in high-energy events, their introverted counterparts draw energy from within. Just to clarify: shyness is different than introversion. Shyness is a product of fear or anxiety in social settings, whereas introversion is simply about a source of energy.

This basic tendency to find energy from within comes out in these observable characteristics of introverts. See if any of these resonate with you:

Embrace solitude Introverts need and want to spend time alone. At work, they prefer quiet, private spaces and like to handle projects on their own or in small groups.

Think first, talk later Introverts think before they speak. Even in casual conversations, they consider others' comments carefully and stop and reflect before responding. They know how to use the power of the pause.

Hold emotions inside Introverts are seldom outwardly emotional or expressive. They can be difficult to read and thus their feelings are frequently misconstrued.

Focus on depth Introverts seek depth over breadth. They like to dig deep—delving into issues and ideas before moving on to new ones. They are drawn to meaningful conversations as opposed to superficial chitchat. They know when to tune into others and when they don't need to spend so much energy doing so.

Let their fingers do the talking Introverts prefer writing to talking. On the job, they opt for email over the telephone and are likely to prefer writing reports over giving presentations.

Act low-key Introverts are usually quiet and reserved. They tend to speak softly and slowly. They have no desire to be the center of attention, preferring instead to fly below the radar. Even in heated conversations, they tend to project calm on the outside.

Keep private matters . . . private Introverts are anti-"open book." They keep personal matters under wraps, sharing information with only a select few; even then, only after they know those people well and feel a level of comfort with them. They can be equally cautious about work matters and stay quiet about their ideas and alliances.

These traits are not good or bad; they just *are*. Unfortunately, in modern society, they are frequently misunderstood, under-valued, and underappreciated. Certainly, they are not usually identified as key drivers of influence. Yet ironically, these traits are precisely why introverts often make the best influencers of all—even in a world that has, until now, assumed that you had to make a lot of noise to make a lot of difference.

Chapter 2

The Six Strengths of Quiet Influencers

"One indication of influence is the ability to stand boldly against hostile trends and thereby alter them."

Madeline Albright, Former US Secretary of State

Time magazine's April 18, 2012, edition profiled one hundred of the most influential people in the world. The write-up included this insight: "Before microphones and television were invented, a leader had to stand in front of a crowd and bellow. Now she can tweet a phrase that reaches millions in a flash. Influence was never easier—or more ephemeral."[4]

Clearly, the nature of influence has changed with technology. But at its core, influence is still about "the capacity or power of persons to be a compelling force on or produce effects on the actions, behaviors, and opinions of others," as *Webster's* dictionary defines it.

I believe that influencers make a difference by challenging the status quo, provoking new ways of thinking, effecting change, or inspiring others to move forward.

Influencers labor in every type of workplace, from soundstages to hospitals. Their jobs range from administrative assistants and authors to parents and community activists. Sometimes, they hold traditional positions of power: they are our most inspired political leaders, academics whose life's work it is to birth new concepts, bosses who motivate people and harness resources, and committee chairs who move projects forward. Just as often, however, influencers don't have the big title. They are simply people who encourage change and growth and achievement: the team member who comes up with the great idea, the middle manager who takes a project to fruition, the colleague who has a knack for changing the boss's mind, the intern whose favorite restaurant becomes the new team lunch spot.

The truth is people who use their natural talents and learned skills to influence others take our world forward in large and small ways. Some of those people are extroverts, some are introverts who make a difference through a process I call Quiet Influence.

Who Are the Quiet Influencers?

Tim Cook, who became CEO of Apple in late 2011 after the illness and ultimate death of Steve Jobs, had some big shoes to fill. His thoughtful demeanor and low-key style were very different from his predecessor, and in his previous role as COO, it appeared that he provided a tempering, calm counterbalance to Jobs's sometime bombastic personality. As COO, Cook was responsible for some major operational changes at Apple that contributed to tremendous company results.

Since his esteemed colleague's passing, Cook has moved forward with his own leadership agenda and has received high marks from many in the technology community. A reporter at Fortune *magazine described an investor meeting in which Cook exhibited his own brand of Quiet Influence. "What shocked the Apple investors that day was that CEO Tim Cook popped into the room about 20 minutes into Oppenheimer's (the CFO) talk, quietly sat down in the back of the room, and did something unusual for a CEO of Apple: He listened. He didn't check his email once. He didn't interrupt.*

After the CFO finished, Cook, at that point chief executive officer of Apple for all of five months, stood to offer his remarks. He strode confidently to the front of the room and held court in the no-nonsense style that has become his trademark. 'He was in complete control and knew exactly who he was and where he wanted to go,' says one of the investors. 'He answered every question head-on and didn't skirt any issue.'"[5]

Would you tag Cook as an introvert? I would. He sat in the back of the room, not needing to be the center of attention. He portrayed a no-nonsense style, which focuses on depth. Yet despite his very quiet persona, he is clearly a powerful influencer. By choosing to make a difference using his quietly effective style, Cook is helping to provoke new ways of thinking and move his company forward. Cook is influencing this incredibly creative and successful company to move past the loss of its iconic founder and forge a new future based on continued innovation. For these reasons, I call him a Quiet Influencer—a person who brings about change and forward momentum in a classic introverted style.

Like other Quiet Influencers, Cook has a personal style grounded in humility. Jody Wirtz, managing director at a commercial bank and one of the Quiet Influencers interviewed for this book, displayed a similar tendency for humility when he answered the question "Do you see yourself as an influencer?" with: "You would have to ask those around me. But if I am an influencer, it is because it is through thought that I have discovered truths and became able to articulate or demonstrate those truths in a way that resonated with others and that eventually worked for them."

Even though humble, Cook and Wirtz are not alone in being recognized for their effective form of influence. Eleanor Roosevelt, Charles Darwin, Mahatma Gandhi, Abraham Lincoln, and Rosa Parks were also introverted influencers. So are Warren Buffet, Condoleezza Rice, Steven Spielberg, J. K. Rowling, and Mark

Zuckerberg. Although many books have been written on the techniques and approaches to influence, they tend to extol a more extroverted approach to influence that presents significant barriers for introverts. Strategies focus on winning people over to your side by putting yourself at center stage, talking things up, presenting great arguments, and verbally convincing others to do what you want them to do. Quiet Influence is not about talking a great game to win the deal. It is a less understood approach to influence and differs from more "out there" talkative methods.

Quiet Influencers can certainly be found where you may expect to find them: in technology, engineering, and science. But they also are found in marketing, project management, teaching, medicine, the law, human resources, and small businesses. Quiet Influencers sell products and services. Nonprofit organizations that compete for funding and airtime also have great movers and shakers who are Quiet Influencers. What they all have in common is that their powerful approach draws upon what introverts do naturally. I have named this approach the *Quiet Influence Process.*

The Quiet Influence Process: Combining the Six Strengths

Through observation and interviews with numerous Quiet Influencers, I have identified the six strengths that introverts embrace to achieve an impact:

1. Taking Quiet Time

2. Preparation

3. Engaged Listening

4. Focused Conversations

5. Writing

6. Thoughtful Use of Social Media

Figure 2.1 The Quiet Influence Process

Each strength, by itself, is a powerful lever of influence; when put together, the power of the strengths multiplies. Introverts typically combine the strengths into The Quiet Influence Process shown in Figure 2.1. More or less sequential, it starts with Taking Quiet Time. Quiet Influencers begin their influencing journey where they think and recharge best: in quiet. Being silent provides energy, increases self-awareness, and spurs creativity. Introverts return to quiet time frequently in order to recharge and reflect.

Next comes Preparation. Careful preparation gets Quiet Influencers ready for all types of situations by increasing their knowledge and poising them to address potential objections. Through creating a strategy and asking questions, they become more comfortable and confident in their efforts to influence others.

The synergistic strengths of Taking Quiet Time and Preparation combine to form a strong core for the other strengths.

With the confidence that comes from tapping into these fundamental strengths, Quiet Influencers move forward out of their own heads and into interactions with others.

They then bring one or more of the next four strengths to bear on the situation. They may tap into their innate strength in Engaged Listening to build rapport and mutual understanding. Or they may decide to engage in two-way, one-on-one, or small-group interactions. These Focused Conversations are purpose-driven dialogues in which they problem solve and work through conflicts with others. Another path they take uses their natural strength of Writing. Through this specialty, they articulate authentic, well-developed positions to make a difference with others. Finally, Quiet Influencers consider how social media platforms can advance their cause. They draw upon their strength of Thoughtful Use of Social Media to reach a previously untapped, broad, or distant audience.

Because they tend to have patience and perseverance, Quiet Influencers don't need to follow the most direct route to an outcome. Although the strengths fit together in the order described, Quiet Influencers often loop back and forth, returning to Taking Quiet Time and Preparation to rebuild energy or confidence, going back to listen for more information to adapt a plan or feed their ideas, or alternating between the verbal interaction offered by Focused Conversations and Writing.

Keep in mind that to succeed as a Quiet Influencer, you don't have to be good in all Six Strengths. Every Quiet Influencer mixes these strengths in different ways according to his or her own personality, needs, and situation. In other words, the Quiet Influence Process is not a formula that requires equal measures of each strength in each case.

Chapter 3 includes a quiz that will help you assess your Quiet Influence Quotient (QIQ), a measurement of how effective you are at using each of the Six Strengths. In the subsequent chapters, you will then explore each of those strengths. You'll read stories, gain practical tips, and even learn when too much of a strength can become a liability.

If you enhance your own quiet strengths, you will make a difference by challenging the status quo, provoking new ways of thinking, effecting change and inspiring others to move forward in ways that magnify who you are and bring forth your passion. Passion does not have to be expressed with fiery words and expressive body language. It can also be a fire burning within. For Quiet Influencers, that internal blaze sparks the courage, creativity, tenacity, and drive that underpin influence. As you read the stories and quotes in this book, keep an eye out for various forms of passion that ignite the Quiet Influencers' desire to make a difference. In chapter 6, for instance, you'll meet Elisha Holtzclaw, a pediatric oncology nurse. She expresses the inner fervor so common to Quiet Influencers when she said, "I love my work and it is in my heart. It is because I have a heart that can handle it. This is my calling."

May you tap into your own heart, your own strengths, and answer your own unique way of making a quietly powerful difference.

Let's get started.

Chapter 3

Your Quiet Influence Quotient (QIQ)

"What I want most to do is be influential."

Philip Johnson, Architect

Would you like to know how well you perform as a Quiet Influencer? Start by taking this quiz to determine your Quiet Influence Quotient—your "QIQ." This tool will let you know how effective you are at using each of the Six Strengths and give you a way to assess your progress as you apply the ideas in the book.

Based on actions that demonstrate the strengths that set Quiet Influencers apart, the QIQ will also give you an idea of how much you have in common with highly effective Quiet Influencers. Assess yourself by indicating how often you engage in these behaviors, using a scale from 1 (never) to 5 (almost always). A caution: Try not to overanalyze the questions. Your initial response is usually the most valid. Also avoid being too tough or easy a critic. Instead, when you respond, be as objective as possible.

1. I take time to be quiet each day.	**1** Never	**2** Rarely	**3** Sometimes	**4** Often	**5** Almost Always
2. I effectively tune out distractions.	**1** Never	**2** Rarely	**3** Sometimes	**4** Often	**5** Almost Always
3. I use my quiet time to engage in self-reflection and planning.	**1** Never	**2** Rarely	**3** Sometimes	**4** Often	**5** Almost Always
4. I develop clear plans to achieve my influencing goals.	**1** Never	**2** Rarely	**3** Sometimes	**4** Often	**5** Almost Always
5. I conduct research as preparation for influencing.	**1** Never	**2** Rarely	**3** Sometimes	**4** Often	**5** Almost Always
6. I adapt my plans to respond to changing conditions and responses.	**1** Never	**2** Rarely	**3** Sometimes	**4** Often	**5** Almost Always
7. When listening, I act as a sounding board for others.	**1** Never	**2** Rarely	**3** Sometimes	**4** Often	**5** Almost Always
8. I tune into another's voice and body language to understand their message at a deeper level.	**1** Never	**2** Rarely	**3** Sometimes	**4** Often	**5** Almost Always
9. I ask focused questions that help people to move forward.	**1** Never	**2** Rarely	**3** Sometimes	**4** Often	**5** Almost Always
10. I use conversations as a vehicle to problem solve with others.	**1** Never	**2** Rarely	**3** Sometimes	**4** Often	**5** Almost Always
11. I share relevant personal information during conversations.	**1** Never	**2** Rarely	**3** Sometimes	**4** Often	**5** Almost Always
12. I make an effort to schedule one-on-one conversations, whether face-to-face or by phone.	**1** Never	**2** Rarely	**3** Sometimes	**4** Often	**5** Almost Always

13. I consider the receivers' preferred communication style when writing to them.	**1** Never	**2** Rarely	**3** Sometimes	**4** Often	**5** Almost Always
14. I put effort into my writing when communicating my position.	**1** Never	**2** Rarely	**3** Sometimes	**4** Often	**5** Almost Always
15. I pay attention to details like grammar, spelling and punctuation when writing to influence.	**1** Never	**2** Rarely	**3** Sometimes	**4** Often	**5** Almost Always
16. I make thoughtful choices about which social media platforms are right for me.	**1** Never	**2** Rarely	**3** Sometimes	**4** Often	**5** Almost Always
17. I actively engage in dialogues through social media applications, contributing ideas as well as reading others' postings.	**1** Never	**2** Rarely	**3** Sometimes	**4** Often	**5** Almost Always
18. I use social media to initiate and/or support relationships.	**1** Never	**2** Rarely	**3** Sometimes	**4** Often	**5** Almost Always

How to Score and Interpret This Quiz

Total the numbers you circled. The following ranges reflect a rough estimate of your QIQ.

Caveat: This is not a scientific or "normed" instrument. Instead, it is a quick self-assessment tool that will help you see which of the strengths you use most often, which could use some development, and how you fare overall. Use it as a guide and starting point as you collect ideas from the book.

If your Total QIQ is	Consider yourself . . .
76–90	**Very Strong** You are using many of the strengths of highly effective Quiet Influencers. Take a look at how you can apply your strengths to some current or upcoming workplace challenges and situations.
61–75	**Solid** You are doing well in demonstrating Quiet Influencing strengths. Some areas still could use some attention. Pinpoint the times when your influencing efforts are successful and not successful. See if you recognize any differences in your use of the Six Strengths in both situations.
46–60	**Moderate** You have some work to do in ramping up your Quiet Influence strength portfolio. Pay attention to a work situation where you are not being effective and consider which different strengths you can apply that you don't typically use.
45 and below	**Lots of Room for Improvement** You have some work to do in living up to your Quiet Influence potential. Start by noticing your own behavior and asking trusted co-workers for honest feedback and suggestions. Begin by working on one strength that you want to develop and set a specific goal for this week. Next week, tackle another skill. Keep at it, you will see results.

Next take some time to compare how often you draw upon each individual strength to influence. Figure 3.1 identifies which questions correspond with which strengths. Add your responses related to each Quiet Influencing strength across the rows in Table 3.1. You may want to create a bar chart to compare the six subscores.

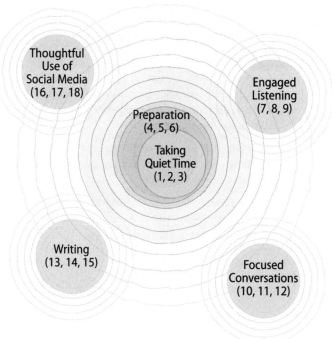

Figure 3.1

Table 3.1

Strength	Score to Include	Score to Include	Score to Include	Total of Scores on this line = QIQ Sub-Score for this Strength
1. Taking Quiet Time	Q1	Q2	Q3	
2. Preparation	Q4	Q5	Q6	
3. Engaged Listening	Q7	Q8	Q9	
4. Focused Conversations	Q10	Q11	Q12	
5. Writing	Q13	Q14	Q15	
6. Thoughtful Use of Social Media	Q16	Q17	Q18	

Use this guide to understand what each of the subscores mean:

If your sub-score on a strength is	Consider youruse of this strength . . .
12–15	**Very Strong** You excel at this strength. Look for ways to apply it to your influencing challenges. Also think about how you can use it to feed other strengths that may not be as developed.
10–11	**Solid** You are doing well in demonstrating this strength. Build on your success by applying it in a variety of new influencing opportunities.
6–9	**Moderate** You have some work to do in developing this strength. Pinpoint the times when you use it with ease and see if you can identify what stops you from using it at other times.
5 and below	**Lots of Room for Improvement** Your low use of this strength is likely holding back your ability as a Quiet Influencer. Consider making it a top priority in your development plans. Watch and learn from effective Quiet Influencers around you who are comfortable using this strength.

How to Use Your QIQ as
You Read *Quiet Influence*

Don't be overwhelmed by the QIQ assessment—and certainly not by your score. It was your first self-assessment snapshot. You have barely gotten into the book yet! Just take it as a clue as to where to put your energies. Remember that you do not need to excel at all of the strengths, all of the time. Before you read chapters 4 through 9, take a look at the subscore in the QIQ Assessment that corresponds to the strength covered. If it's very strong or solid, review the chapter with an eye to expanding the ways you already use this strength. Pay particular attention to the Overuse section to make sure that you're not turning an overuse of a strength into a weakness.

If your subscore was moderate or showed lots of room for improvement, consider investing significant time on that chapter and the included advice and tips. Pay particular attention to those lower-scoring strengths that appear in your job description or that you know to be important in your job. For instance, if you are in sales, chances are that Engaged Listening and Focused Conversations are priority strengths for you. If the people you interact with are dispersed across a large corporation or all around the globe, the strengths of Writing and Thoughtful Use of Social Media will probably rank higher on your list.

No matter which strength or strengths you identify as your development priority, you'll discover many useful ideas in this book, especially in chapters 4 through 9, where you will collect specific actions to act on today. These actions will enhance that strength. Regardless of which area you decide to address first, use the following additional tips to keep you moving towards an even higher QIQ:

Look for places to practice   Once you have highlighted an influencing strength to work on, look for opportunities to apply that skill. Here's an example: If you believe you may be missing out on voice and body language cues to understand peoples' messages at a deeper level (question 8 on the quiz), consider your schedule and identify times when you might practice being more observant. The grocery store line, the gym, and walking to work all then become laboratories for observation and learning.

Give yourself a pat on the back   After you try on a new approach, give yourself a big "atta boy or girl." It's always hard to go out of your comfort zone, and you should recognize yourself for taking that first step, even if it didn't feel natural or have the desired consequences. Build on that feeling of accomplishment.

Recognize what is working   Acknowledge when you have mastered a skill. Such recognition gives you a launching off point. Most likely, these higher rated strengths come more naturally to you. Keep using them to make an impact and remind yourself of those assets, especially those days when influencing feels like a chore.

Ask others for feedback   You will accelerate your growth as a Quiet Influencer if you ask for and receive feedback from others who see you on a regular basis. Make it easy for people to help you improve by telling them what to look for. Let's say you want to strengthen your writing. Consider asking a "QIQ buddy" to give you honest feedback on what was unclear in an email or proposal. You can only improve a skill when you know how you're doing. Feedback will also reinforce your progress and build confidence.

Be aware of reactions   Notice how you feel when you incorporate a new influencing strength. For instance, focused conversations may be uncomfortable at first if you usually influence people through writing. Be aware of the influencing results you are getting from your new behavior. Likewise, observe how others react. For instance, when you begin to initiate conversations, your co-workers might be surprised and maybe even a little wary. Usually, it takes only a little bit of time for everyone—including you—to adapt.

Your Next Steps

The advice in this book will be even more meaningful to you if you apply it to a specific influencing challenge you now face. Before going further, take some quiet time to reflect on the following questions and record your answers. I'll be prompting you to think about this challenge as we go along.

1. Is there a situation at work in which you would like to have more influence? Take some time to describe it here.

2. Who is or are the key players involved?

3. What two or three main challenges do you face in this situation?

4. What actions or behaviors have you tried so far? What results have you seen?

5. What would be a satisfying outcome to this situation? How would things be different from how they are now?

6. Review your QIQ scores. Which one or two Quiet Influence strengths might you try applying to this influencing challenge?

No matter the level of challenge you face, in today's workplace, Quiet Influence will increase the impact of your work, give you more deserved visibility, and bring high value to your organization. Your relationships will deepen. The investment you make in sharpening these strengths will have payoffs now and in the future.

But take it one step at a time. Let's start where the Quiet Influence Process starts. It's also where you are likely to enjoy your most thoughtful moments in the day or most idea-rich time of the week: during your quiet time.

Chapter 4

Quiet Influence Strength #1:
Taking Quiet Time

"What a lovely surprise to discover how unlonely being alone can be."

Ellen Burstyn, Actress

Julie Irving is an administrative professional who supports more than sixty people at the Battelle Energy Alliance, a contractor for the Idaho National Laboratory in Idaho Falls, Idaho. Julie won the prestigious American Management Association's Administrative Professionals Innovation award in 2009 for voluntarily creating

and executing a car blind-spot safety program for her company and the wider community. It has reached more than ten thousand adults and children at regional and local events.

The educational safety program Julie conceived and implemented has certainly influenced others and saved many lives. Her motivation to pursue her journey came in the form of a potentially tragic car accident involving her daughter. Julie said, "One day I received a phone call from my daughter. She told me that she had been involved in an accident. Now, nobody was injured in the accident, but it seemed quite unbelievable. You see, she told me that she was backing up her Dodge Durango and backed into a 'monster truck.' I asked her why she didn't check her rear- and side-view mirror's before backing up, and she said, 'I did, but I couldn't see it. It was in my blind spot.' Now, I have great trust in my daughter but have to admit that this story seemed a little hard to believe. So I decided to get online and do a little research on back-over accidents. What I discovered led me down an incredible road that not only changed my life, but touched thousands of other lives as well."

Realizing the lack of national attention to car blind-spot safety, she relentlessly pursued her crusade. Julie started by researching blind-spot safety online. She found a video that showed a couple of vehicles lined up with an array of props placed behind them. The video demonstrated how the drivers were unable to see those props. Intrigued, Julie set up her own simulation. She placed props behind her own vehicle every ten feet up to sixty feet. When she then sat in her vehicle and properly adjusted the rear and side-view mirrors, she was shocked to discover that neither the ten-speed bicycle nor the tricycle that she had just placed thirty feet behind her were within her view!

Julie shared this newfound information with her own family but wanted to do more "in hopes of preventing a tragedy." She developed posters and family awareness booklets. Additionally, she created an interactive blind-spot safety presentation, which *she presented alongside her organization's safety team first, to hundreds of coworkers then at a regional conference. She then took the presentation to the broader community. Together with volunteer trainers she ultimately reached more than ten thousand adults and children.*

Although her daughter's accident inspired her, the seeds of her influential work were planted under the stars during the quiet moments she gives herself at the end of the day. Julie recalls, "I am always mentally exhausted by the end of the day. I really look forward to my quiet time. It is essential to my being able to recharge. . . . My quiet time usually comes in the evening, when I've completed what I feel to be the most important things that I needed to accomplish for that day. I finally take the time to unwind and rejuvenate, usually in the hot tub." She went on to say, "My quiet time is also my time to think, think and think . . . dream, plan, face frustrations, and then work through fears and issues. I have found that during this time, I often come up with original thoughts and ideas, explanations, or answers that I had not considered before. . . . Looking at the stars and the heavens is always refreshing and makes me smile." And, it seems, doing that also inspires her to make a big difference here on earth.

How do you find and use your quiet time? How do you escape from the jarring static of texts, emails, and the "Do you have a minute?" conversations that interrupt you from your best thinking just as it emerges? Blaise Pascal, the French mathematician said, "All men's miseries derive from not being able to sit in a quiet room alone." In fact, studies show that meditating—perhaps the most intense form of conscious quiet time—brings down blood pressure and slow breathing reduces anxiety. And that's important because stress, distraction, unhappiness, and anxiety can keep you from being the best influencer you can be.

If you want to increase your total QIQ, begin by prioritizing quiet time and using it to your best advantage. Ironically, you improve your ability to influence others by finding a time and place to be *away* from others. As an introvert, you need solitude—or at least time away from actively interacting with others—to perform at your peak. You're probably well aware that you want and need to spend time alone. Introverts suffer from people exhaustion and are more sensitive to various kinds of stimulation, including noise, movement, and light. Because it lays a solid foundation for each of the other strengths, Taking Quiet Time is the first strength we'll delve into. Remember, even though it is most often the first step Quiet Influencers take, quiet time is also an energy-restoring retreat to which you can return again and again throughout the influencing process.

Taking Quiet Time and Influence

Taking Quiet Time contributes to your ability to influence others because it unleashes your most creative thoughts, sustains your energy, increases your understanding of yourself and others, and helps you maintain focus.

1. Unleash Creativity

When you prioritize quiet time, you increase your ability to tap into your knowledge, skills, and experience in order to solve problems and develop ideas. Influencers, by definition, promote new ways of thinking. Quiet time allows these innovative ideas to percolate and then emerge from your mind. Your right brain, the side that is more unstructured, experimental, creative, visionary, and less orderly, has a chance to work to a fuller capacity when you are in a relaxed state. The ideas that set you apart as an influencer—the ones that cause people to stop and listen—are nurtured in these moments of solitude.

In fact, new research reveals that the best ideas emerge from solitude. Susan Cain, author of *Quiet: The Power of Introverts in a World that Can't Stop Talking*, writes that solitude is actually a catalyst to innovation because it has long been associated with creativity and transcendence. She mentions that creative geniuses such as Steve Wozniak, builder of the first PC, naturalist Charles Darwin, and author Madeleine L'Engle all cultivated their dreams during quiet time.[6]

Science journalist Sharon Begley would agree. Writing in *Newsweek*, she noted, "Creative decisions are more likely to bubble up from a brain that applies unconscious thought to a problem, rather than going at it in a full-frontal, analytical assault. So although we're likely to think creative thoughts in the shower, it's much harder if we're under a virtual deluge of data."[7]

Quiet Influencers report seeing this phenomenon in action. Former salesperson and now executive coach Vinay Kumar explains how quiet time contributes to his version of creativity: "Most of my writings emerge from someplace deep within during moments when I am jogging, hiking, *et cetera*. . . . Those are the times my subconscious mind seems to be most active."

2. Sustain Energy

Introverts recharge by spending time alone, often with reduced sensory input. As an introvert, you need solitary quiet time in order to be present and your best with people. If you are worn out, it's difficult to be present enough to challenge the status quo and inspire others to move forward. Rebuild your energy by stepping away from the action for as much time as you need and can take.

Writers are influencers who provoke us to think differently through their words. Many are introverted and have learned to conserve their energy for the often draining task of writing. Author Stephen King, for instance, reserves his mornings when his energy is highest for serious writing. "Mornings are for my new novel. Afternoons are for naps and letters. Evenings are for reading, family, Red Sox games on TV, and any revisions that just cannot wait. Basically, mornings are my prime writing time."[8]

There's no doubt that this schedule has helped King influence millions of readers with his prolific and diverse work.

3. Increase Your Understanding of Yourself and Others

When you use your quiet time for calm reflection, you get to know who *you* are. You become more self-aware when you take time to allow your thoughts and feelings to emerge. You can assess your motivations, tap into your values, recognize your strengths, and address your weaknesses. Keen self-awareness means that you can make better choices about how you influence others and react to others who try to influence you.

One influential CEO of a successful media company shared that he often has his influence-related "breakthroughs" on his fifteen-minute walk from the bus stop to his office. "I figure out how I will approach a situation and how I will frame the conversation. I may decide, for instance, that this time I don't have to be assertive and can let the conversation flow and the dynamic emerge."

As this example illustrates, calm reflection during your quiet time also gets you ready to interact most effectively with others. If you're always stimulated, in constant action, or incessantly interrupted, you'll find it hard to really think about other people and see life from their perspective. But in your own space, you are able to consider the position of other people before you engage directly with them.

Ann, a senior paralegal for a leading fashion house, walks for exercise and quiet time. On one walk, she made the decision to connect with a "highly aggressive co-worker" by asking about her young son. These conversations brought them to common ground and proved to be a turning point in their relationship—one that opened up an avenue of influence for Ann and helped her unglue a sticky project. In short, because of a decision she made during quiet time, Ann was able to lead this powerful woman to consider new ways of thinking by developing rapport and trust with her.

4. Maintain Focus

Taking Quiet Time—even if it is just a few concentrated minutes—can sharpen your focus and effectiveness so that you can best challenge the status quo and influence situations and outcomes. Take for example Adam, a former ski racer. He started the sport at an early age and, by the time he reached college, was skiing with the likes of Olympic champion Bode Miller. Adam explained that before every race, he visualized each and every turn. He could see the entire run clearly in his mind before he left the gate. When it came time to perform, he had already been there in his mind.

Adam performed this focusing exercise during the quiet time he took right before competing. Today, as a management consultant, he uses that same approach in quiet conference rooms on project sites. Before client briefings, he runs over presentations in his mind. Just as he did back on the ski run several years before, he anticipates the twists and turns ahead. He visualizes tough questions and potential push back, deciding in these moments how he will respond. Through the focus he develops in quiet time, Adam has developed an enormously effective low-key, persuasive influencing approach that results in his clients often taking the actions he proposes.

Taking Quiet Time to focus is also essential for Jane, a program manager at the Centers for Disease Control and Prevention (CDC). She deals with outbreaks of infectious diseases and says that "everything is urgent because you could be saving lives and you always feel like you are flying a plane . . . and . . . building it at the same time." In one situation, she was trying to figure out how to win the buy-in of another department. Before a session with a small peer-coaching group, she quietly mulled over ideas in her head. Then she was ready to engage with the coaching group to discuss potential solutions. This initial step of mental preparation helped her to focus the discussion. Jane ended up using the group's input very effectively to solidify her case.

As described here, focus is a form of mental preparation that's part and parcel of the other kinds of preparation covered in the next chapter, chapter 5. One Quiet Influencing strength naturally blends into another, but only by prioritizing quiet time can you undertake this kind of mental preparation.

How to Take Quiet Time in Order to Influence

Quiet Influencers use a variety of highly successful approaches to obtain their quiet time and turn it into a zone for calm reflection. There is no one right way to recharge and reflect, and no two introverts interviewed for the book have precisely the same approach to stepping away. Many do so by creating structure to protect their quiet time, managing technology, and going within themselves.

1. Create Structure and Protect Your Quiet Time

Schedule and protect quiet times on your calendar Make a date with yourself as important as your appointments with others. Consider the experience of Wally Bock, who calls himself a "borderline introvert." A personable leadership coach and prolific writer, he swears by solitude. When discussing the option of joining writers' groups, he laughingly said that he isn't a "flocker." Bock explained that he would rather write than talk about writing. Each morning, he schedules three hours to write and he invariably plants himself at his desk. He methodically writes blog entries and posts them on social networking sites. He influences others by engaging with people online and promoting his colleagues' ideas. Wally recently surpassed blog post number one thousand and has more than nine thousand followers on Twitter. Now, that's a lot of influence that emerges out of scheduled quiet time!

COMMUNAL SOLITUDE

Ava, a sophisticated city-based sales rep, hosted her counterpart Lauren, who came from a small town. During the rounds of calling on customers, they stopped at the local Starbucks. It turned out that Lauren had never been inside one of the ubiquitous stores. As they left, Lauren asked Ava what all those people were doing "with laptops and earphones." She wondered why they would go to a gathering place and not gather. Because engaging in the activity of quiet, communal solitude was second nature to her, Ava was surprised at the question. She explained the "alone but together" concept to her perplexed partner.

Quiet time doesn't necessarily have to involve physical isolation. Sometimes, that's not possible. And, in fact, many introverts get some of their best work done in the company of others. They don't have to be talking to them. In a coffee shop, for instance, the energy of other people, the forced focus, and the choice of whether to engage in the action heighten the experience of quiet time. Like group meditation or sitting communally in a library, simply being in the company of others can provide an unexplained comfort that builds confidence and allows people to go deeper into self- and other-awareness.

Get up early   Like Stephen King, you can use the morning to get a head start. Sophia Dembling, a popular blogger and author of *The Introvert's Way*, has had more than two million views on her *Introvert's Corner* blog. She said, "I work alone, so finding quiet time comes very naturally.[9] In fact, I find a lot of quiet time! I had houseguests last week . . . and so sometimes in the morning I wouldn't get out of bed right away. Instead, I'd bring my computer into bed. And I just would spend a little time by myself before I got up and faced them. I adore these people, but it was a lot of people!"

Keep eating lunch alone   Do you feel guilty for eating lunch alone? Don't. These breaks give you the opportunity to be with yourself. Using your midday break to regroup and recharge can be an ideal strategy, especially if you don't do it every day. Take for example David, an executive who works at a software company. He says that he always dines alone on days that involve a lot of time in front of people. By having a book in front of him, he says he wards off friendly would-be visitors.

Build in breaks   Because being "out there" can be so draining, be sure to take yourself out of the office, away from the conference, or removed from wherever work happens to be—if only for a few minutes. Even a short walk outside or down the hall will make a difference. You will find yourself returning to your influencing role refreshed and re-energized.

Select your optimal working environment   Think about where you are most effective. With technology and company practices allowing more latitude as to where and when work gets done, you may have more control over your environment than you assume. A flexible work environment can provide the quiet time you need. Try negotiating for home-based work a few days a week, or, if you work in an open-plan office, book a conference room for time by yourself.

2. Manage Technology

Turn off your devices   Go ahead. Try it. Push that off or silent button during your quiet time. Wait until later—preferably a planned time—to turn it back on. Even for introverts, it can be extremely challenging to set aside certain times to check electronic devices. Yet ongoing interruptions become huge distractions when they break up the blocks of time you need to think and create. It is commonly thought that it takes from four to fifteen seconds to get back on track from every email interruption. Find applications (apps) and software programs that help you manage this issue. These programs can schedule your social

---

HOW ONE ORGANIZATION SUPPORTS QUIET TIME

Microsoft's New Way of Working Program exemplifies how an organization has recognized the need for its employees to have quiet time. All employees at the software giant's office outside of Amsterdam have home offices but also come in for meetings and collaboration.

When researchers at the Rotterdam School of Management measured the impact of this program, they found 40 percent improvement in work/life balance scores over five years and measurable improvements in productivity. The report said: "Now, no one has a fixed office anymore and the building has been designed to be what we call activity based. It is no longer an office in the traditional sense. Instead it is a workspace where employees can locate themselves in different parts of the building depending on the tasks they need to perform. Increasingly, it is a meeting place where employees can interact with colleagues, partners, and clients."[10]

Because this balanced approach provides options that respond to the preferences of both introverts and extroverts, it promotes an environment that encourages thoughtful, purposeful, communication and nurtures creativity and decision making, the hallmarks of influence.

---

media postings, turn off Internet access after a set period, and even manage what lands in your inbox.

Reduce stimuli Adapt your environment to foster quiet time. Introverts often dim the lights and use white noise machines to drown out the cacophony and create a calm, quiet atmosphere. If stimuli interfere with your quiet time, avoid noisy restaurants and crowded places; opt instead for the quiet of your home or a hidden corner of a park.

Turn off all sound   Try taking a walk without headphones and driving with the radio off. Use earplugs or noise-canceling head-phones on a plane. Just being quiet allows your brain and body to take a much-needed rest so that you can restore your energy and let the creative thoughts flow in. A few years back, I took an Amtrak train from Baltimore to New York City. After a long day, I settled into my seat on the crowded car and immediately noticed that something felt different from past excursions on commuter trains in the Northeast. What was it? Suddenly, it struck me. No one was shouting into a cell phone or engaging in loud chatter. I looked around and noticed people dozing, dreaming out the win-dow, reading, writing and simply zoning out. I had landed in the middle of the "quiet car!" I enjoyed a beautifully peaceful ride and arrived at Penn Station rejuvenated and more ready than ever to use my influencing skills to hail that elusive taxi.

3. Go within Yourself

Exercise   Get up and move around. Quiet time doesn't have to be sedentary time. In fact, exercise is an essential component of many people's quiet time. Josh, a thirty-something operations manager at a Fortune 100 company and introverted father of three, seems to handle his many responsibilities with ease. Where does he get the energy to influence in all the ways he does? Josh said that he squeezes in a workout whenever he can. After those mini-breaks, he finds himself more focused. He says, "It's kind of . . . resetting, recharging my battery." His active version of quiet time provides some of the fuel for the influence he has demon-strated through bringing innovative programs to his organiza-tion's business resource groups, writing Japanese language books for businesspeople, and leading cross-cultural training programs to help improve communication with overseas call centers. He even has added graduate school to his list of vibrant activities.

Keep a journal   Capture your thoughts, insights, dreams, joys, and worries in a notebook or computer. The process of writing, which is Quiet Influence Strength #5, brings clarity to your thinking and serves as a kind of meditation. Former salesperson and executive coach Vinay Kumar said that when he tries to force his thoughts, nothing happens. But when he enters his quiet time, ideas flow. As Vinay humbly explained, "I don't think I have the brains to come up with a lot of the stuff I write. Thoughts just come out of nowhere. And for me, unless I write—until I write them down—they keep coming up over and over again. And the minute I can write them down, they are gone and then new thoughts surface in my mind." As a former salesman and executive coach, Vinay is an advocate for introverts and challenges conventional thinking by writing encouraging words to the many introverts in his community. Likewise, writer Randy Peterson emphasizes the importance of having the right tools when he settles into quiet time. "When I want to be creative, it's time for the classical music, a yellow pad and a fountain pen—not a ballpoint—sitting by the fireplace, and I just sketch things out. Something about the smell of good ink," he muses.

Don't forget to breathe Shake out the kinks in your body, take a good stretch, and focus on your breath. Consider counting "1, 2, 3" on each inhale and exhale. You will become more aware of your breathing and inevitably ease into quiet time. Purposeful breathing also helps you stay in the present moment. You forget about what happened yesterday and what waits for you tomorrow. With conscious breath, you are able to stay focused on your best and deepest thinking.

Take naps Find an appropriate time and place to take a daytime doze. Many successful influencers swear by power naps because their subconscious works best during sleep. David, the software executive, explains the link this way: "I am considered an introvert, and I am transitioning to a leadership role. My position requires a lot of public speaking, training, and facilitating meetings. Often, I will withdraw after long meetings or training sessions. I take two-hour naps to recharge."

Overuse of Taking Quiet Time

Overuse of any strength can translate into a weakness. Life is about balance. That's why taking *too much* quiet time can negatively impact your ability to influence others. Specifically, too much quiet time can lead to ideas that languish, lack of motivation, lost perspective, and lost opportunities.

1. Ideas that Languish

When you take too much quiet time, you can generate so many ideas that you end up in a form of creative paralysis. The ideas that emerge might be brilliant. Yet if they remain within you and you and do not move any of them into action, they remain just that: ideas. Millions of books remain unwritten and innovations continue untapped because their originators stayed in quiet time instead of moving out to share these ideas with others.

2. Lack of Motivation

Batteries need only a certain amount of time to recharge. Any time past the point of full charge becomes self-defeating and yields no positive effects. Even though each introvert needs a different amount of quiet time, most agree that overuse of this strategy ends up depleting their energy. It can even lead to isolation and even depression.

Take for example a common challenge facing the long-term unemployed, a group I have worked with through several recessions. I found that when these potential job candidates spent too much time at the computer sending out résumé after résumé, they lost energy and motivation. When they volunteered their services to others, however, their sadness diminished, they moved away from a focus on their problems, and they became re-energized. Having too much quiet time to focus on their predicament clearly did not motivate them and that time at home drained the energy they needed in order to influence an employer to hire them.

3. Lost Perspective

Although being aware of your strengths and blind spots can help you be an effective influencer, staying inside your head too much can be self-defeating. You end up second-guessing your decisions, questioning your abilities, and delaying action. All in all, you can lose perspective and erode your ability to make a difference and effect change.

How much introspection is too much introspection? Keep this helpful phrase in mind as you considering how much self-awareness is enough: "Look back but don't stare." When you realize that you are simply recycling the same thoughts and not learning anything new about yourself, it's time to stop the mental music. Getting stuck in self-analysis can plant you too firmly in the act of dredging up of the past—an action that rarely helps you move on to productive action.

4. Lost Opportunities

Staying parked in solitude can also contribute to lost opportunities to advance yourself and your cause. Here is how it works. Something called the "perception gap" kicks into gear; that is the difference between how you want to be perceived and how you are actually seen. Let's say you spend a lot of time alone at work on your projects. Unfortunately, "out of sight and out of mind" rings true in most workplaces. When you are not visible, co-workers may decide you are aloof, snobby, or angry when this is not actually true. Unfortunately, this misperception can lead to strained working relationships and your ultimate ability to influence others.

Consider this example: A university administrative office had a staff of six people. Five withheld important information from the sixth named Jaya. The staff assumed her closed door meant she was not interested in their discussions. But the opposite was true; Jaya needed that information but she also needed downtime. Not having that vital information affected Jaya's ability to influence her faculty constituency. Unfortunately, her need for privacy led to the staff's false assumption that Jaya was disengaged. That was not at all her intent. When both parties honestly aired their impressions, they cleared up the disconnect and were able to figure out a way to share important information with each other while still respecting Jaya's need for quiet time.

Another way too much quiet time can lead to lost opportunities is an overreliance on the vision you create during quiet time. Relying too heavily on a specific outcome can throw you off balance when the real scene unfolds. Life in the real world is never exactly as we imagine it. Multiple scenarios can occur and you don't want to get so wedded to your view of events that you are unable to go with the flow. Sarah, a purchasing agent, imagined winning over a team leader on her proposal. She pictured everything about the pitch meeting and replayed the successful scene in her head multiple times. Unfortunately, at the actual meeting, she was interrupted by questions from a guest expert who had been invited at the last minute. Sarah was thrown off guard, lost her cool, and swept up into an anxious place, leaving her unable to truly listen to what was being asked. In the end, she lost her opportunity to sell her proposal.

Your Next Steps

Taking Quiet Time *isn't* a luxury only a few can afford. It *is* an essential way to take care of yourself so that you can have the most impact in your work and home life. If you already find and use quiet time, stick to it. And if you don't dedicate time to yourself in this way, give it a try. It will help you with each of the other Quiet Influencing Strengths and form the foundation for a strong QIQ.

Start ramping up your commitment to taking quiet time by focusing on these five main points from the chapter:

1. The ideas that set you apart as an influencer often emerge from solitude.

2. Even a few concentrated quiet minutes can sharpen your focus and effectiveness so that you can move action forward and challenge the status quo.

3. Change some habits to make quiet time a priority. Try eating lunch alone and recharge by building in breaks, exercising, or taking naps.

4. To make the most of quiet time, turn off your technology devices.

5. Remember, too much quiet time can deplete your energy and keep your great ideas locked inside your head. Take your quiet time and then return to the world to influence people and situations.

Next, deepen your learning by reflecting on these questions:

1. When recently did you take quiet time to think through a problem, issue, or opportunity? If you took quiet time, were you able to calm down or see the situation in a new light?

2. Where can you go without distraction to reflect and plan? What activities provide you with good reflection time?

3. How might taking some quiet time help you with the influencing challenge you are facing now—the one you identified in chapter 3?

Taking Quiet Time is good for you, your QIQ, and ultimately your organization. But what do you do with the clarity, energy, and focus that emerge from quiet time? You apply it to fuel the next core Quiet Influencing Strength, Preparation.

Chapter 5

Quiet Influence Strength #2: Preparation

"Intuition is critical in everything you do but without relentless preparation everything you do is meaningless."

Tim Cook, CEO, Apple

Jake is an introspective associate director of English for a large educational nonprofit organization. Recognized as a highly effective manager, Jake fits the bill as a Quiet Influencer. The Quiet Influence strength that has become his signature quality: Preparation.

Take how he handled this challenge as an example. In the testing phase of a new teacher-training program, Jake needed to convince a significant number of regional partner agencies to persuade their teachers to use new and improved materials. He faced two key obstacles: one, the fact that the agencies and teachers already felt overloaded, and two, the risk these partners perceived about getting on board before the program was finalized. Most agencies said they would rather wait until all the kinks were ironed out before investing the time and effort necessary to launch a new curriculum.

Jake thought carefully about these objections and crafted a plan to convert these regional agencies into critical development partners. First, he created a short teaser video with animated stick figures. It was poignant yet humorous so that viewers could relate to the issue and presented the problem that needed solving. Jake distributed the video to a wide range of new and potential partner agencies. Next, he discussed his vision for the program in one-on-ones with key opinion leaders within the regional agencies. After a sneak preview presentation, Jake asked them to each submit a proposal for consideration as a tester.

Each of these steps built excitement and began to provoke a new way of thinking about what it meant to get involved with a pilot program. Jake and his boss then worked through the challenges and together identified action steps so that the regional agencies could start moving forward.

"In the past, we've primarily asked our senior leadership to choose a regional partner," Jake explains. "By opening the opportunity up to everyone, this process felt more democratic and allowed regional teams to generate their own enthusiasm. . . . It made them feel more invested and eager to access this resource before everyone else—even if it wasn't yet perfect. They became more convinced that working with us would be a good idea. As a result, I didn't have to do as much up-front convincing because by the time we sat down to meet, they were already fairly certain

that this program was something they wanted to pursue, and it
would put them a step ahead of other regions."

Does Jake's careful, well-thought-out preparation remind you of how you would approach an opportunity or overcome challenges? A trademark strength of introverts, Preparation is especially useful for influencing people. Although their more extroverted counterparts excel at "winging it," Quiet Influencers rarely skip the Preparation step. They spend quiet time reflecting on their purpose and then create a game plan and influencing strategy that incorporates attention to detail and a steady, disciplined approach to change.

Ultimately, this methodical, strategic approach makes a huge difference in an introvert's ability to influence others. Preparation often dovetails with Taking Quiet Time. Together, these two strengths form the core from which the other strengths grow. If your total QIQ needs a boost, consider concentrating on Preparation because this strength can feed your performance in the other areas. And if your subscore for Preparation was lower than you'd like, don't be tempted to skip to a different strength first. Start here or with Taking Quiet Time because until you really pay attention to Preparation, you can't really perform the remaining four strengths effectively.

Preparation and Influence

Critical to your success rate in influencing others, Preparation helps you to become an expert, prove the value of your proposal, involve others, and increase your confidence.

1. Become an Expert

Quiet Influencers know what they're talking about. Why? Because they do their homework and take the time to learn about their subject. For example, when a job candidate prepares by taking the time to learn about the industry, company, and job, the hiring manager can't help but be impressed. Mollie, an administrative professional, interviewed with an Asian Studies college department chair. She made sure to read about his research interests before their conversation. She asked one question regarding the evolution of modern Chinese families, and the interview dialogue was off and running. A job offer followed soon after.

With characteristic patience, Quiet Influencers realize that effecting change is not a one-time event but a multi-step, layered process that requires keeping up-to-date on their subject. Insurance salesperson Ashley knows that it takes time and careful preparation to understand and truly team up with a colleague, client, prospect, or potential partner. She shared, "The time when I make the sale isn't when I have the proposal in my hand. The sale is made over the years. . . . If you know your stuff and bring something of importance to prospects; they are going to value your time with them. They will engage you at some point." Her team's twenty-year track record of successes is proof that this strategy works.

2. Prove the Value of Your Proposal

Introverts take the time to gather pertinent facts so they can present a very strong case for a new way of thinking or course of action. Derrick, a senior editor at a publishing company, plays an important role in selecting which books make it through the rigorous selection process. He conducts extensive research before making book recommendations. He researches magazine articles, policy papers, the Internet, and other sources to find corroboration for his argument. When taking a contrary position, this third-party evidence helps him to challenge the status quo and address his publication board's resistance. Because they know he comes to publication meetings well prepared, his colleagues respect his judgment and listen carefully to his well-crafted positions.

Another Quiet Influencer, Jody Wirtz, is a managing director at a commercial bank who acknowledged that he is "not a natural born salesman." Instead of relying on flashy presentations, he proves the value of his ideas through two threads of research. First and foremost, he analyzes his customer before trying to convince him or her to buy a product. "An idea, product, or solution may not be right for everyone. No matter how good you are, you will never convince a Nordstrom shopper to begin shopping at Wal-Mart and vice-versa." The second way he proves the value of his product: understanding what makes his idea, product, or solution different from others. That means doing some competitive research and thinking through how he will convey his product's relative strengths and weaknesses. When he takes time to prepare to prove the value of his products to a specific audience, he typically makes the sale.

3. Involve Others

Few Quiet Influencers achieve their goals alone. Most realize that they magnify their ability to make a difference when they strategically involve others. Not only can extra hands make lighter work, extra minds bring in other ideas and extend your reach. And remember that you engage people precisely by involving them, so the mere act of asking someone for help increases your influence. It takes preparation, planning, and management, however, to involve others in a timely and effective manner.

Sometimes, Quiet Influencers bring in just one other person—the *right* other person—in order to gain traction. In order to win the coveted rights to the sensationally successful *Hunger Games* trilogy, producer Nina Jacobson had to achieve the trust and sign-off of the young adult series' writer Suzanne Collins. After spending a lot of time herself on the phone with Collins and her agent, Jacobson asked a mutual friend, writer and director Peter Hedges, to vouch for her. Jacobson recalls, "Peter, who did *Dan in Real Life* at Touchstone when I was at Disney, had gone with Suzanne to a creative writing program in North Carolina. So I asked Peter to call Suzanne on my behalf and talk about the experience, so she would know when I told her I wanted to have a collaboration with her, I was being honest and it wasn't just lip service." Jacobson's approach worked: she convinced Collins to sell her the rights and she went on to produce a blockbuster that reached millions of moviegoers worldwide.[11]

At other times, Quiet Influencers enroll many people in their projects. Selah Abrams, whom you will meet again in chapter 9, is a low-key thirty-something engineer in a large media organization. But that is only one of his many roles. He has partnered with companies in South Africa to create more than one hundred thousand entrepreneurs in the entertainment industry, initiated a successful chapter of the New Leaders Council, and spearheaded his company's vibrant *NextGen* business resource group for Millennials.

In each of these projects, Selah has forged relationships with what he terms "co-instigators," key players across his organization who are willing to co-sponsor his community service endeavors. Quick to credit others for his success, Selah *never* uses the word *I* when discussing his various projects. "Even if I do more work on something I will always say 'we.' It grates on me when people take all the credit." In preparing for presentations related to these endeavors, he uses a collaborative approach. "I bounce ideas off of other people and always consider if having someone else go along or even be the main speaker would be advantageous." By consistently flying under the radar, Selah effectively uses this engagement strategy to effect change.

4. Increase Your Confidence

Introverts often suffer from the "undersell syndrome": they keep so quiet about their accomplishments that people don't know about the value they have to offer. Their more talkative colleagues often overshadow them at work and move ahead. More than four out of five introverts have said that extroverts get ahead at work.[12] In fact, when introverts are passed over for projects and promotions time and time again, they may start to lose belief in themselves. With the increased inner strength and confidence that emanate from preparation, however, they can enter any situation for which influence is called—particularly those in which they are likely to rock the boat by challenging the status quo.

When they have a well-prepared game plan that builds from their past accomplishments, they feel their confidence build. For many, like the management consultant Adam we met in chapter 4, mental exercises undertaken during quiet time boost confidence. Others get ready for a new challenge by making a list of their recent accomplishments and referring to it as they psych themselves up; it reminds them that they do indeed have what it takes to succeed.

Jean Paul is a salesman in a technology company who finds that he does better in meetings when he takes time to prepare. He says that "knowing what the conversation or meeting is going to be about really helps me do better. . . . Once I have a good comprehension of the subject, I feel a lot more comfortable with the conversation itself." Like a number of Quiet Influencers, he often plays out future conversations in his head in order to gain perspective and confidence. Asking himself how the other person might react helps him deepen his understanding and enter sales calls more confidently. This shift leads to his ability to be really present with his customers, inspiring them to think in new ways about their problems and the solutions he proposes.

Even top executives prepare for influencing by building their confidence. Doug Conant, former president and CEO of Campbell Soup Company, likes to visit venues before meetings and "brings a buddy along for confidence." "My buddy," he explains, "is someone who is knowledgeable about the situation we are dealing with and has the potential to enhance the discussion." Conant refers to this confidence booster as a "touchtone"[13] that allows him to relax and focus on the purpose and content of the meeting.

How to Prepare for Influencing

Because they plan so strategically and consciously, Quiet Influencers can pinpoint exactly how they get ready for meetings, conversations, events, presentations, and other influencing opportunities. Their actions fall into four logical steps that you can follow: gather information and insight, strategize, manage yourself, and practice.

1. Gather Information and Insight

Pull together what you know   Gather information you already have and organize it. The famous introverted movie director and writer Woody Allen keeps pieces of paper with ideas in a box. He pulls out these random notes to get inspired for a project. This nonlinear way of preparing works for him, and there is no doubt he has influenced millions of people with his provocative movies.[14] Where is your "idea box"? Is it in your Outlook Notes, in a simple file folder, inside a bedside notebook, or on your smart phone's recorder? An idea box can take any form: find one that is right for you.

Conduct "due diligence" before meetings   Businesses undertake due diligence (research or analysis done in preparation for a business transaction) all the time in order to know exactly what they're getting into. Quiet Influencers, who also like to know what they may face in a given conversation or meeting, use their preparation time for due diligence too. Often, their approach involves reading files and information packets and speaking to people in the know. Jake, the associate director of the nonprofit we met in the chapter opening, is a big fan of due diligence. "I like to have as much information and context as possible before a conversation or meeting: What might the other person be hoping to get out of the conversation with me? What assumptions, knowledge, or questions is he or she already likely to have, and how can I elicit that information early on?" He uses this information to finalize his preparation: "I like to create clear agendas. . . . I like to have a pretty clear idea of what we're going to talk about, why, and in what sequence."

If your influencing opportunity involves a meeting or a presentation, conduct due diligence to clarify the meeting's purpose beforehand. Jake shares: "If the conversation or meeting is a request for my feedback or requires that I have certain background knowledge, I ask for written documents that I can review in advance whenever possible so that I can take time to process my thoughts before we talk."

Do a deep dive Expand your knowledge of a topic by finding and absorbing new information. Singapore-based senior producer, presenter, and radio personality—and introvert—Michelle Martin reads and researches every book she covers on her popular and influential show. "If it is an author I am interviewing, it goes without saying that I need to dive deep into her books. It would be disrespectful to her and her work if I didn't." Her intensive prep results in provocative questions that bring out more than superficial answers from her guests. In turn, Michelle's large radio audience responds to the often-controversial discussions that emerge.

You can take a deep dive by conducting Internet searches on a topic, reading published articles, speaking with people who have knowledge of your topic, and visiting places related to your influencing mission.

2. Strategize

Interview yourself Conduct a question-and-answer strategy session in your head. What you are trying to accomplish? Do you want to change the world with a mission that's important? Raise broad awareness for an issue? Generate funds for a cause you believe in? Also consider who you are trying to reach. Take a guess at their objectives and imagine how they might respond to what you bring to the table. Once you identify those basics, you

PREPARING TO LEAD A MEETING

When you chair a meeting, you step into a perfect place of influence. Make it most effective for all involved and increase your influence by following these meeting preparation tips:

1. Decide if there should even be a meeting. Figure out if you can solve a problem or communicate information using alternative approaches like one-on-one focused conversations (see chapter 7). Al Pittampalli, author of *Read This before Our Next Meeting*, calls meetings "weapons of mass interruption." He says a leader's most important decision is when to call a meeting and when not to do so.[15] Thinking through your method can save time, cut costs associated with people and time and improve your ability to impact others.

2. Select an appropriate time, place, and agenda. Schedule meetings at times when participants are not rushed or tired. Find spaces that are inspiring, comfortable, and conducive to the kind of work you need to do. Match the agenda to the time available and include breaks and plenty of time to stretch. Introverts will appreciate the time to recharge their batteries, and extroverts who want to keep talking will meet up spontaneously on their own.

3. Expect that people come prepared. Although you may not control your company's culture, you do control how you conduct your interactions. If you expect people to prepare for a meeting by reviewing materials and reflecting on the topic, send out agendas and background information well in advance. Tell attendees that you expect them to read these items before (not during) the meeting. If they arrive unprepared, suggest rescheduling the meeting. At first, people may think you're going overboard by creating an agenda and setting high preparation expectations. Know that people will get used to it and that you're in good company. The semiconductor company Intel long ago insisted every meeting must have an agenda. No agenda, no meeting.

continues ▶

4. Prepare mentally, physically, and technically. Get on conference calls early to establish rapport and work out any technical glitches. Arrive at a physical meeting early so that you can recharge before leading others. Save time to set up the space. Consider assigning seats for optimal interaction. An introverted marketing director said she changes her seat when she wants to lessen one of her strong team member's power positions: the times she wants to show who's boss, she sits directly across from him.

will know how to channel your preparation efforts. You can also distill from your self-interview a list of "LAQs" (Likely Asked Questions) and prepare answers for them.

Draft a strategic plan Jot a few lines on a sticky note or create a formal plan. Your written plan should be as involved as the situation. Jody Wirtz, the managing director we met earlier in chapters 2 and this chapter, prepares for internal meetings by listing a three- or four-item agenda and drafting introductory and concluding remarks that frame his position. Karen, a research librarian, advises thinking through the objective you want to achieve and the points you want to make. She formulates her own conclusions and next steps prior to any meeting.

Prepare for your own meetings by crafting talking points and questions that are relevant to the session. You will do the best job at this task when you know the role you are playing, why you are there, and your goal. Quiet Influencers who seek to effect major change on a wide scale often produce very extensive written influencing project plans such as the kind described in the box on the next page.

Think of alternative scenarios Prepare to navigate the inevitable twists and turns that come your way. Despite careful preparation, you can't always anticipate what will be thrown at you. Radio

---

DEVELOPING AN INFLUENCING PROJECT PLAN

When you want to make a big difference or tackle a complex challenge, write an "influencing project plan." This document will help you solidify your goals, keep on track, and involve others. Dave Basarab, author of *Predictive Evaluation*, suggests thinking through your idea using this model: [16]

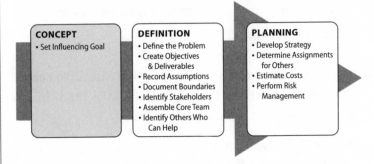

CONCEPT
• Set Influencing Goal

DEFINITION
• Define the Problem
• Create Objectives & Deliverables
• Record Assumptions
• Document Boundaries
• Identify Stakeholders
• Assemble Core Team
• Identify Others Who Can Help

PLANNING
• Develop Strategy
• Determine Assignments for Others
• Estimate Costs
• Perform Risk Management

Is the time you spend putting together your plan worth it? Basarab says yes. "People who take the planning phase seriously achieve their goals, plain and simple. And they do so with less stress than those who make things up as they go along. Winging it may work for the small stuff, but when something is really important, there's no substitute for proper planning."

---

personality Michelle Martin deals with uncertainty every day. "Each show is exciting to me because I look at it as collaboration: a dance where the guest, listener, and I all shape what happens. There are many unknown elements—guests can stall at the mike, callers can turn rude, or one of my mind-maps can go missing. My goal is to try to roll with the flow."

Dealing with what happens in the moment sometimes trumps preparation. Take for example introvert Meryl Streep's acceptance speech at the 2011 Golden Globes ceremony. In the blush of winning and kissing her way up to the stage, she forgot her glasses and couldn't read her prepared speech. So how did she handle it? She was refreshingly real (the producers bleeped out the "Oh ____"), cracked some jokes, and complimented the other nominees (some even more than once). Her rambling, laughing speech showed a real performance that probably won over even more fans than she already has.

3. Manage Yourself

Pause   Take the slow-but-deep approach to influencing. Remember to use your natural strength of responding thoughtfully and patiently. Instead of trying to avoid the normal and necessary resistance you'll encounter as you try to influence change, take a breath and take it in stride. Give yourself time to think before writing an answer to potentially charged emails. Try sending a draft copy to yourself and then edit or delete it. Calm down when you feel the heat rising in conversations. You'll win when you maintain your composure and wait to respond until you have settled down.

You will definitely be more effective at creating and using pauses when you tap into quiet time and allow yourself "breathing room" during your day. Switching between thinking tasks takes time for introverts. Writer Sophia Dembling leaves herself plenty of time and space between appointments. She arrives early and says she would much rather sit in her car in a parking lot to regroup and relax before meeting with people than rush into a meeting. Education administrator Jake concurs: "Regardless of the call or meeting topic, the time of day, or the person I am meeting, I take a few minutes in advance to review any previous notes to refresh my memory." Closing your eyes for a slow, relaxed visualization can also be helpful during these preparatory pauses.

Positive self-talk   When faced with conflict or a difficult challenge, ask yourself the question, "What would I do if I weren't afraid?" Create a good cop/bad cop scenario. For every negative thought or assumption you tell yourself (that's your bad cop), refute it with a positive, good cop thought. So when you find yourself thinking something like "Management won't take my idea seriously," consciously switch the message to "I have an innovative, worthwhile idea that will help our organization."

Ask for help Avoid exhaustion and burnout by knowing your limitations and enlisting the help of others. Successful Quiet Influencers have overcome their reluctance to ask for assistance. Amelia, an accountant, learned the importance of this from the interns she was managing. They were not shy about asking for help and their questions helped to move the project along. So, when faced with her own work overload she took a lesson from their playbook. Amelia met with her own boss, and in five minutes he helped her prioritize her many tasks. Steered back on course, Amelia learned that asserting yourself when you need help goes beyond even saving time. It also shapes others' perceptions of you as a proactive influencer who challenges the status quo (for example, her workload) when things are getting off track.

4. Practice

Learn your lines Stand up and give your influencing remarks a test drive. Dr. Walter May, an assistant dean at a liberal arts college, admits that public speaking doesn't come naturally to him, so he rehearses extensively. At least a week before every speech or presentation, Walter pulls out a music stand at home, gets his posture right, and practices what he is going to say. When he goes "live," his points are well articulated, and his message impacts the many students and faculty members in his audiences. Experts often suggest this kind of practice. "Rehearsal is the art of experimentation," says presentation skills coach David Greenberg.[17] Try experimenting by recording your influencing remarks, even if they are only the opening of an expression. You will find yourself using words and expressions that are different and often more impactful than those on the written page. You can incorporate them into your next presentation.

Find your voice Experiment with different tonalities of your voice. Although you may be aware of the impact of your body language (eye contact, posture, etc.), you may not have given much attention to your voice. Voice expert and author of *Full Voice*, Barbara McAfee, says you should vary your vocal sounds. Different situations demand different tones of voice, she explains. For instance, to make a serious point to a serious person, you may want to move down to your deep "earth voice." At times when you want to arouse excitement, it makes sense to tap into your passionate "fire voice."[18]

Create two versions of every pitch Prepare specific pitches to correspond to the situations you're most likely to face. Often, you will not end up with the amount of time you really want to present your ideas. Josh, the busy operations manager and father of three who uses his workout time to recharge and gain quiet time, suggests having a short and a long version of what you want to present. "I prepared an hour and a half pitch to a senior vice president who then said, 'Okay, I need to cut this meeting short and you have three minutes to convince me!'" That experience taught Josh about always having a short form of his pitch in his hip pocket.

Overuse of Preparation

The amount of preparation you need depends on the scope and importance of the situation you want to influence—and how naturally you are able to exert Quiet Influence. Sometimes, you can indeed prepare too much. As you develop your own set of Quiet Influencing strengths, you'll learn what level of preparation is right for you and when you need to step away from preparation to enter the moment at hand. These cautions about getting stuck in the preparation rut will help you find your own balance. Overuse of Preparation can lead to analysis paralysis, lost connections, lost focus, and sabatoged confidence.

1. Analysis Paralysis

When does preparation become too much preparation? When nothing gets done. At a certain point, you just have to get out there and do it. Too much time spent gathering or checking your facts keeps you stuck in inaction, blocked from getting out there testing your ideas and gauging reactions. Ideas don't get adopted without a give and take. Part of the influencing process is floating ideas and hearing the push back. Don't be tempted to keep researching out of fear that you'll miss an important fact. You will never be able to find all of the relevant facts, you will never be able to predict the success of a change you propose, and you will never know for sure what will stand in the way of challenging the status quo. In short, perfection is a tough goal to reach, and you don't need to have all the facts. Shoot for 80 percent.

Software engineers, for instance, have to learn how to gather enough, but not too much, input from customers. When they go overboard in collecting data, their final product risks being late to market, over budget, or obsolete. In addition, at times their customers don't really know what they need, so spending an inordinate amount of time questioning them doesn't necessarily result in the best product possible.

2. Lost Connections

When you focus your preparation so intently on proving your own case, you may go into a conversation, meeting, or presentation so focused on your own message that you miss the opportunity to tune into the needs and desires of your audience. Overpreparation sets you up to stick to the script in a way that may not allow you to really hear others' concerns and points of view. Every second you spend thinking about getting back to your plan is a second of lost listening. You may miss out on important nuances of body language that can help you tailor your message in the right way. You will lose connection with the very people you hope to influence.

Radio personality Michelle Martin sums up the danger of overpreparation succinctly: "When I first started I would try to script every question. That was tedious, and though I may have sounded very commanding, I bored myself! After twelve years in radio, I have learned to give up needing to know how each show is going to turn out. The best shows happen when I am able to respond in the moment, and there is a sense that my guest, the listener, and I have each had a chance to participate and help it unfold the way any good conversation does. If I didn't prepare ahead of time, I would be too anxious to let go and let 'live' radio just happen!"

The loss of connection due to overpreparation is particularly poignant in presentation settings. Today's audiences don't have much patience for the "sage on the stage." Though people still want to hear from an expert, they also want to be engaged with a dynamic, interactive speaker. How do the content or ideas apply to their own situation? Material takes on more relevance and application when they can discuss it, ask questions, and spend time in vibrant and challenging discussions. Wise college professors and professional speakers have heeded this lesson.

3. Lost Focus

Sure, involving others can increase your reach and your resources. In fact, most people are willing to be involved precisely *because* they want to be part of the change or action. For that reason, be sure to keep your focus on the end goal rather than the process of getting there. Take for example a volunteer organization that held an event to assemble personal hygiene bags for the elderly. The planning committee prepared intricate assembly stations, games to introduce volunteers to one another, and other team-building activities. In the end, the actual number of bags assembled fell significantly short of the desired goal. Why? The committee had not ordered enough toiletry supplies to complete the task. Spending so much time trying to engage the team meant the focus of the preparatory phase was taken off the end goal. Such a mistake can mean the difference between successful or failed influence.

Alexis, a public health officer, learned a similar lesson. She wanted her team to cooperate more without her direct intervention, so she organized and planned a very structured meeting that forced them to work together in groups. Many resisted this approach. As luck would have it, collaboration did occur. It wasn't, however, as a result of her planning. It happened informally outside of the formal meeting agenda, during walks and at lunch. At first, Alexis was disappointed that her plan hadn't worked. It took her awhile to realize that the meeting had achieved its purpose. Alexis learned that her tendency to overplan and her insistence on group participation almost blinded her to the fact that she had accomplished her primary goal of instilling collaboration.

4. Sabatoged Confidence

Sometimes, too much of a focus on developing confidence through preparation can backfire. Overpreparation can create anxiety and cause you to lose your footing. For instance, as you research a subject in order to build your case and commitment to influence others, you may realize you don't know as much as you thought you did. Or perhaps you become less sure of your position as you learn more. Both scenarios can be confidence busters.

Too much preparation can also keep you "too much in your head," concerned about what you will say, what you are saying, and what you just said. In considering situations like this, one interviewee shared, "I lose words and then lose my train of confidence, which makes me frustrated." This faltering can have a snowball effect and make you come across as insecure in your position—not a good place to be for influencing others.

In *The Introverted Leader: Building on Your Quiet Strength*, I laid out the 4 Ps process: Prepare, Presence, Push, and Practice. You'll notice that Prepare is just one step of this fluid process. You can prepare only up to a point before the second-guessing and doubt move in to replace confidence and motivation. It is important to move on and to be present with other people in your change efforts.[19]

Your Next Steps

Chances are, Preparation comes naturally to you. Because Preparation feeds the strengths of Engaged Listening, Focused Conversations, Writing, and Thoughtful Use of Social Media, attending to this core strength is a terrific way to increase your QIQ. To get started, first consolidate what you've learned in this chapter. Here are five highlights:

1. Careful, well-thought-out preparation is a trademark strength of Quiet Influencers.
2. Quiet Influencers are often experts who have conducted extensive research on a subject.
3. The right amount of preparation sets you apart. Too much preparation, however, can kill your confidence.
4. Few Quiet Influencers achieve their goals alone. It takes planning to involve others.
5. Quiet Influencers often develop written plans that provide a road map for the influencing journey.

Take your commitment to Preparation further by mulling over these questions:

1. Think of a recent time when you successfully proposed an idea at work. Did your preparation for the conversation or written proposal pay off? What aspects of preparation were most successful?

2. Think of another time when you weren't as prepared as you would have liked. How effective were you as an influencer? What do you wish you had done differently in terms of preparation?

3. What steps can you take to prepare for the influencing challenge you identified in chapter 3? Would you benefit from a written plan? Do you want to involve others in planning or implementing your influencing strategy? If you answered yes to either of these questions, how and when are you going to follow through on those aspects of preparation?

Often, Preparation involves gathering and processing information. One way Quiet Influencers do that is through Engaged Listening, which is Quiet Influence Strength #3. In the next chapter, you'll learn how Engaged Listening can not only feed your Preparation but also build connections with other people—connections you'll use to further your influencing goals.

Chapter 6

Quiet Influence Strength #3: Engaged Listening

"The greatest compliment that was ever paid me was when someone asked me what I thought and attended to the answer."

Henry David Thoreau, Philosopher

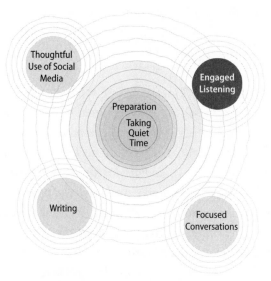

Elisha Holtzclaw is a pediatric oncology nurse at Children's Healthcare of Atlanta at Scottish Rite. When talking with Elisha, it becomes apparent why everyone from the chief nursing officer to her peers rates her so highly; one described her as a "quiet soul with a great influence on patients."

Elisha listens attentively and closely to patients and their families. Her calming presence and empathic, tuned-in approach encourages them to share their feelings and questions. The result? Elisha helps move them forward to make what may be the hardest decisions of their lives.

This anecdote demonstrates her tremendous listening skills in just such a situation. A young terminal patient was just a few weeks away from death. Elisha had become a trusted confidant to his mother as she traveled the course of his treatment. One day, in the outpatient clinic's infusion room, the child slept after having received pain medication. In this private, quiet, dimly lit space, the mother sat in a reclining chair and Elisha sat on the bed, rubbing the patient's leg to comfort him and listening to the mother to comfort her. Intently focused, Elisha looked into the mother's tearful eyes and empathetically maintained a connection to her pain. The mom asked, "Be honest with me. I know that you will. Please tell what you would do if you were in my shoes right now. Would you go for hospice or press on for treatment?"

Elisha recollects, "I was as honest as I knew how to be, and I tried to picture myself in her shoes. I told her that if I felt my child was dying from cancer and suffering in pain, I hoped I could make the best decision. I explained how hospice can add to the comfort of home. He would have his family and me by his side without having to leave home. And when the time did come and he took his last breath, I would want to be right there and see him gain his angel wings and go peacefully in comfort." The caring and compassion that came through in Elisha's answer carried the mom through the impossibly hard decision to take her son home.

This heartbreaking story makes us think about our own ability to truly listen. Do you listen well enough to develop deep empathy with others? Through listening, do you, like Elisha, earn the opportunity to influence? To speak and be heard when your input really matters?

If you are like most people, you may not be nearly as good a listener as you might think. Studies show that poor listening is a leading cause of conflicts, misunderstanding, and low performance. And yet, those same studies demonstrate that listening is a vastly underrated skill.

That's the bad news. The good news is that introverts—who, let's remember, make up 50 percent of the population—are natural-born listeners. In fact, introverts are more likely to listen to and process the ideas of an eager team in a deeply engaged way. Introverted leaders actually influence their more talkative teams to achieve higher levels of performance than more extroverted leaders do, according to recent research.[20]

Listening to words and "listening" to body language through observation help you learn about the people and situations you are trying to influence. Consultant and author of *Getting to Resolution: Turning Conflict into Collaboration* Stuart Levine suggests that by truly listening "You allow each person to get their story out on their table, define the problem space, validate everyone's position, and reveal everyone's interests."[21]

That openness and validation set the conditions for trust. Quiet Influencers like Elisha listen their way into trusted relationships. Because they tend to effect change from a place of trust, Quiet Influencers work hard to earn that trust and don't take it for granted. They are unlikely to use their position of influence for short-term gain because they know they are in it for the long haul. Quiet Influencers reject bait-and-switch influencing tactics and avoid promising results they cannot deliver. They are driven by their internal convictions and are uneasy with tactics that could jeopardize the deep relationships they have worked hard to develop. For all these reasons, they put Engaged Listening at the top of their to-do lists.

As an introvert, your Engaged Listening strength can be leveraged to make an impact on people and processes. When you take the quiet time you need to prepare, you ready yourself for the challenging task of truly listening. Through listening, you may gain a much deeper understanding of the situation at hand and then choose to return to Preparation. Fine-tuning your Engaged Listening skill will also help you increase your total QIQ because it enables effective two-way focused conversations (Quiet Influence Strength #4) and can lead to insights that you can carry forward in Writing (Quiet Influence Strength #5) and Thoughtful Use of Social Media (Quiet Influence Strength #6).

Engaged Listening and Influence

Engaged Listening contributes to your QIQ and your ability to influence by helping you to increase your understanding of situations, deepen your empathy, gain credibility, and build engagement.

1. Increase Understanding of Situations

A primary way to bring in information and insight, Engaged Listening helps you understand what's going on around you: what people are thinking and feeling, threads of themes, and even what key pieces of the puzzle might be missing. Quiet Influencers often find that the process of asking open-ended questions and then listening to the answers without judgment surfaces important clues to influence. When carefully tuning in and listening to others, you can pick up ideas to help you plan your next steps and influencing approach.

Melinda Gates, head of the Gates Foundation, has been listening to women in Africa for a long time. A May 2012 *Newsweek* article described her approach to visiting foundation-supported vaccine programs in sub-Saharan Africa. "Gates would often ask women at remote clinics what else they needed. Very often, she says, they would speak urgently about birth control. 'I was just stunned by how vociferous women were about what they wanted,' she says. Because of those women, Gates made a decision that's

---

ENGAGED LISTENING TO MAKE THE SALE

Like *The Music Man*'s Harold Hill, salespeople have a reputation for being fast-talking showmen who don't listen. Yet introverts can make very successful salespeople precisely because they tend to be good listeners. Here are some ways that Engaged Listening can help you make the sale:

Listen for pain points. When you know what is of concern to customers (expenses, profit, quality concerns, fear of changing to a new provider, etc.) you can probe further to get to the real root of their concern and show how your service or product can help them solve their key problem.

Ask open-ended questions such as, "Tell me . . . what's happening in your world?" or "What is standing in the way of you reaching your goal?" When they answer say, "What about _____ concerns you? Can you give me an example?" Through engaged listening and probing in this manner, you'll really understand the problem before recommending a perfect customized solution.

Listen to people while they "tell their story from beginning to end," as author Stuart Levine suggests. When you take that time, you gain a more complete picture of their position and their needs.

Ask for and listen to their feedback. Former salesperson and now executive coach Vinay Kumar asks questions like "How am I doing?" and "What more can I do for you?" Then he listens very carefully to the answers without responding then and there. The answers tell him what to sell to his prospects and how to do it. You gain client respect when you make adjustments based on such feedback.

---

likely to change lives all over the world: she decided to make family planning her signature issue and primary public health priority. 'My goal is to get this back on the global agenda,' she says."[22]

Ann, the senior paralegal introduced in chapter 4, said, "It's amazing that when you listen to a group of people together in a meeting, you can really tell a lot about them." In one particularly contentious project meeting, she listened carefully in order to learn who the dominant players were and how they interacted with others; Ann kept that knowledge in mind when meeting with them individually and was well prepared and confident. Her subsequent approach was critical to winning them over.

2. Deepen Empathy

When Quiet Influencers like Elisha in the opening story show empathy, they listen in a way that lets people feel truly heard. Empathy is the ability to understand the thoughts, feelings, or emotions of others. When you demonstrate empathy for the people you want to influence, you truly understand them as human beings; their motivations, aspirations, joys, worries, and points of pain. You are also able to understand their points of resistance and why they hold onto the positions they do. Empathy building and engaged listening aid in developing a connection between people, and they set the stage for further helpful conversations.

Tricia, a young engineer, was frustrated that an older man she worked with named Ken had little interest in revamping a purchasing process to make it run more efficiently. She was not making much progress in getting her ideas heard until she decided to bring some empathy into the situation. When she listened to Ken with her whole self, she realized that he was being driven by a fear of change and a concern about learning new technology. After gaining this awareness, she was able to inspire Ken to move forward by addressing each of his concerns.

Because of their tendency to be great observers, introverts have exceptionally alert radar for picking up on subtle cues about a person's deep feelings. The best Quiet Influencers simply have a knack for learning to read and interpret a look or a shrug. In preparing to portray the role of Nelson Mandela in the film *Invictus*, actor Morgan Freeman studied Mandela up close. "You have to watch and listen," he explained. His close observation felt, in his words, like a "direct transfusion from the man himself."[23]

Quiet Influencers can even develop a type of telepathy with another person. Elisha hypothesizes, "Because I am quiet and a good listener, the other person can feel what I feel." From her point of view, such empathy contributes to less static and clearer communications, and it ultimately opens up pathways to inspire others to move forward, even with the most difficult decisions of their lives.

3. Gain Credibility

Listening to people in an engaged way and taking their words to heart are important in effecting change. For instance, when you make a commitment to research a concern and then actually get back to the person with your response, you increase your credibility with that person and other people they impact. Building credibility is a process that happens one intentional action at a time.

Tran, a trainer for a government agency, wanted her class of engineers to step out of their comfort zones and to be open to some new leadership approaches. First, however, she needed to gain "street cred" with the group. Why would they listen to her when, in their minds, she knew little about what they did on the job? Tran approached this obstacle by asking for written input at the end of each day of her five-day class. Her targeted questions yielded helpful input. Simply listening to their needs demonstrated her sincere desire to learn more about their situations and where their management skills were faltering. Before the start of each session, she read the feedback and asked for even more clarification to help her zone in on the topics to emphasize in her class. This engaged listening process built Tran's credibility with the students. They were very receptive to learning and gave the class unusually high marks. Moreover, they went back to their teams with new, practical approaches they could apply immediately. Tran had made a difference in their leadership performance.

4. Build Engagement

Although influence is sometimes about changing thought patterns, it is often about inspiring others to move forward and take specific action. Others will only take that step when they are engaged with your idea or truly desire the change you present. Much has been written about how to build engagement, and you can find solutions that can be quite complex. Quiet Influencers know that the simple act of engaged listening is often what transforms their personal goal into a shared goal that others want to achieve as well.

In press interviews for *The Introverted Leader*, I found that many reporters wanted to talk about their personal experience with introversion instead of asking me questions about my point of view. When I tuned in to them instead of sticking to my talking points—when I listened and encouraged free-flowing conversation—they inevitably wrote excellent well-thought-out stories that reflected our deeper dialogue and posed new, more provocative questions.

Ironically, a powerful tool for influencing people is silence. Often, a person will talk themselves out of a wrong decision without the listener saying a word. Or as Ben, a department store manager, finds, others—especially extroverts—will often reveal information they would normally not reveal simply because he's not saying anything. He finds this approach particularly useful as he conducts hiring interviews: applicants will frequently share information about their style of working and interests when he listens. This extra insight helps Ben place them on teams where they will be most motivated, engaged, and successful.

How to Use Engaged Listening in Order to Influence

Although there are countless resources that aim to teach listening skills, these introvert-tested tips will help you develop your Engaged Listening skills and raise your QIQ. They fall into four categories: create the right conditions, serve as a sounding board, ask questions, and go beyond words.

1. Create the Right Conditions

Slow down Because of your naturally quiet temperament, you may not need this reminder to slow down and really listen. But chances are you work in a typical organization where things are revved up and due yesterday! This pace may force you to become distracted when you are attempting to tune into a person. You also may move more quickly and adopt some nonproductive behaviors such as interrupting others or rushing a conversation to a quick conclusion. You can be an island of calm amid this storm of activity. Remember that giving others the time to reflect and respond in meetings, conversations, and even in casual chats is a gift that will yield great benefits. Others will feel heard, and you will feel yourself return to your natural pace.

Get face to face Arrange a quiet place to listen and show up prepared to focus. Try to identify a setting or activity that will help someone open up to you. By making the time to convene in a relaxed environment, you not only get to read the other person's body language and voice, you also demonstrate that you care about what the other person has to say. Face-to-face meetings are particularly critical when you are trying to effect change or make a difference. It is helpful to do this at the start of a project to begin building relationships early on. Global teams that function well often make an effort to get people physically together in the same room at least once a year.

Remember also that live conversations don't always need to be scheduled; they can also happen though serendipity. Steve Jobs often took impromptu walks with key contacts. *Wall Street Journal* reporter Walter Mossberg wrote that Jobs revealed some of his deepest thoughts and feelings during these unplanned times.[24]

Use technology to listen to multiple viewpoints   Pose questions to dozens, hundreds, or even thousands of people at the same time through a webinar, a format that offers an excellent opportunity for listening. Your audience's immediate responses, either through spoken words or through answers to instant polls, let you gauge the "temperature" of the group and get a handle on shared concerns and issues. Their questions can also be enlightening and reveal new areas for potential influence. Although such technology doesn't get you face to face with people, you can learn to use it to improve your influence by better understanding what's going on in situations and by building engagement through interactivity.

2. Serve as a Sounding Board

Just be there   Let the other person speak—even "vent"—without giving advice or otherwise interrupting. When you do, others feel heard, are able to sort out their own thoughts and feelings about a situation, become clearer about issues, and thus figure out what steps they need to take. You have invited them into a place from which you can then inspire action. Vinay Kumar, the coach mentioned earlier, said, "Many people bare their souls. . . . I am their safe space where they feel truly heard and understood. And frankly, I don't do much except listen and ask questions. The answers generally surface in due time."

Paraphrase   Reflect back what you hear when you listen. Be sure to say it in your own words and don't parrot exactly what you hear (repeating their words sounds condescending). The very act of summarizing what the other person has said or articulating thoughts in a different way helps you process the information more fully. This also allows you to demonstrate your increased understanding *and* portray your empathy. Just as importantly, you find out if you have heard the information as it was intended. Often a misinterpreted word here and there can morph meaning, so by paraphrasing throughout the conversation, you avoid disconnects down the road.

FOCUS: TIPS TO AVOID BECOMING
DISTRACTED WHILE LISTENING

Although Engaged Listening comes more naturally for introverts than it does for extroverts, it's still easy to lose focus when trying to listen for a long time. Try these tips to improve your concentration:

Don't even try to multitask while listening. Although talking on the phone while driving in the car or walking on a busy street is a natural time saver, such multitasking doesn't give you the chance to truly listen. Try scheduling phone conversations at times when you have fewer distractions so that you can really tune in. PS: Taking and making calls in the public bathroom stall is off-limits!

"Bracket" distracting thoughts. Do you ever find your mind wandering to what you didn't get done at the office, what you're making for dinner, or the fact that you need to call your mom—all while you are trying to listen to someone else? Such thoughts block your ability to really hear the nuances of what the other person is saying. To improve your attention, take those thoughts and imagine placing them in brackets where they can stay safely tucked away while you really listen. They will be there for you when you're ready for them.

Mentally interview yourself. When you listen in an engaged way to someone discuss a subject about which you have little interest, ask yourself questions in your head about the material. Those questions will keep you focused on what you're learning and highlight areas you may want to know more about.

Move your body. Take a cue from the wise judge presiding over a murder trial: every hour he turned to the jury and instructed, "Ladies and gentlemen, please stand up." He explained that he needed them to be alert; sitting too long detracted from the acute listening required of jurors. You, too, can improve your listening by standing up every twenty minutes and moving around while you are talking on the phone or listening to an audio presentation.

Add value   After listening quietly, help the person move out of inertia and toward action. Share ideas, connections, and resources that come to mind. As an introverted assistant dean of a liberal arts college, Dr. Walter May finds that engaged listening lets his students know he is concerned about what they think and feel. It is from this trusted foundation that he influences students, particularly those in trouble. He explains that students "unload traumatic stuff, and I gently guide them toward the services they need." Case in point: a student named Akela had missed more than ten classes over the course of a semester. Through listening to her story, Walter came to understand that Akela was suffering from serious depression. By the end of the conversation, Akela trusted Walter enough to agree with his suggestion that she see a counselor. This major step presented the breakthrough that helped Akela move forward toward eventual recovery. Through engaged listening, he has built trust with so many students that they often contact him years after they have graduated; a data point that his boss calls "proof of his influence."

3. Ask Questions

Prepare questions in advance   Go into listening situations with a set of questions in hand. Introverts tend to prepare their questions before meetings, presentations, and conversations. Take Juan, for example, an introverted plant manager from South America, who transferred to the United States to manage a growing chemical facility. As part of his development, he went through a 360-degree feedback assessment process during which his customers, managers, peers, and direct reports provided perspectives about his strengths and weaknesses as a leader. After the results came in, Juan met with the groups who had participated in the survey. Before these meetings, Juan had made a well-thought-out list of questions designed to help him better understand the feedback. By asking these questions and seriously listening to the answers, he was able to see what he needed to keep, stop, and start doing. Juan's willingness to listen and inquire with intent helped him gain stature and influence with his team and upper management.

Use open-ended questions Gain more insight with questions that can't be answered with a simple yes or no. Open-ended, well-crafted questions yield richer information and allow you to hear the speaker's unique perspective. Most of the best open-ended questions begin with *how* or *what*. Answers to these questions provide the information and deep understanding you need to make a positive impact and move people forward. Jane, the program manager at the CDC, says that she pulls out quieter team members by calling them by name and then posing open-ended questions such as, "Tom, what do you think of this?" In this way she showcases the person's expertise within the group.

Identify a new line of inquiry Through your questions you can influence the trajectory of a conversation. Jane also finds that a group explores new paths of discovery when she listens carefully and asks the right questions. Sometimes, she builds a bridge between two participants in order to let their experience and needs guide the direction of the discussion. She may say something like, "So Bernard, you have been in a similar situation to Fernando. Will you share the lessons you learned?" Writer Sophia Dembling said that in her role as a reporter she finds that interviewing is all about listening to the implications of words. It is not just listening to what others say but also about "what question comes out of it." By really listening, she might find a "whole different and intriguing tributary to take."

4. Go beyond Words

Read their nonverbals Observe the person carefully while you are listening. Nonverbals—the signals people send through their eyes, facial expressions, and body—contribute strongly to the overall message they send. Vinay Kumar, the executive coach, says, "I listen with my whole body, not just with my ears. I listen less for what is said and more for what isn't said. Without intentionally trying, I capture emotions, body language, tone, and undercurrents. All that combined tells me lots more than just what the person is saying through words." When you see or hear mismatches between *what* is being said and *how* it is being said, ask a question to bring focus to the disconnect. When he picks up clues of discomfort from body language, Josh, the operations manager, asks questions such as, "I know you are committed to the timeline, but I see that you look somewhat puzzled. What questions are still on your mind?" Such questions will allow you to probe deeper in order to gain a fuller understanding of where the roadblocks to influence lie.

Be aware of your own Engaged Listening presence Tune in to your own nonverbal signals in addition to observing the eye contact and body language of others. Such signals combine to form your Engaged Listening presence. If you show that you are truly listening, people will feel comfortable opening up. Quiet influencers at Xerox have taught Ursula Burns, the CEO, the importance of having a poker face. She has "tempered outspokenness and calls herself the 'listener in chief.'" She knows that by being a receptive listener she encourages innovation and ideas from her employees.[25]

Hear voices Notice when another person's voice goes up or down, or when his or her speech gets faster or slower in discussing different topics. By tuning in to someone's voice, you are able to understand his or her message at a much deeper level. In her instructive and inspiring book *Full Voice*, Barbara McAfee states that when you learn to align *what* you say with *how* your voice and body say it, you also become a better listener who taps into "what people are saying beneath and between their words." She calls this "deep listening" a "rare and precious skill . . . that transforms both speaker and listener."[26]

Overuse of Engaged Listening

Sometimes, listening too much can stifle your ability to influence. If you are truly listening, you are not, by definition, talking or doing anything other than tuning into the other person. There are times when you can have a greater impact on situations and people by not listening quite so much. The overuse of Engaged Listening can have four negative impacts on your ability to influence: loss of credibility, conflict avoidance, unproductive conversations, and unheard ideas.

1. Loss of Credibility

Asking questions as part of engaged listening certainly helps you gain information and build relationships. Yet in some organizations and cultures, asking too many questions can contribute to a perception that you don't know very much or are not confident about what you do know. Ultimately, you may even lose your ability to share your opinion. At one workplace, Jeremy would consistently ask questions like, "Would it make sense if we tried doing such and such?" He rarely made a statement that put forth his opinion or took a stand. Needless to say, when he did feel strongly about something, most people tuned him out because they were so used to his tendency to never state an opinion.

2. Conflict Avoidance

Listening with empathy is a great way to be supportive. But too much empathy can actually impede action because it can lead to the avoidance of conflict. Soon Lee, an introverted web designer, admitted she, like many introverts, steers clear of conflict. Yet in her line of work, the seeds of creativity are sown in the conflicts that bubble up when artists interact. Though Soon spent a considerable amount of time showing empathy in order to understand the viewpoint of others, that meant she rarely expressed her unique point of view. This hesitancy contributed to the perception that she didn't have much to contribute. In discussing the low rating on her performance review, Soon Lee's boss told her that by not challenging others and focusing so much on making them feel heard, cared for, and comfortable, the department was missing out on her different point of view. Her contrary and unique approaches were needed to create alternative solutions and the best web design ideas possible.

3. Unproductive Conversations

Finding the balance between Engaged Listening and speaking is also tricky, especially if you are a strong introvert who would rather stay silent. When you are a great listener, people feel comfortable talking to you. They may continue to talk on and on, rehashing the same ideas without getting anywhere. It is, however, difficult to solve a problem when the only person talking keeps talking about the problem and not about solutions. As the "listener in chief," you need to make sure that person you're listening to does not become a "venter in chief." If you don't ever ask questions that move toward solutions, you enable others to stay stuck in the problem. When Leila, a quiet customer service representative, senses that it's time to move on from venting, she states what she's heard, then suggests next steps for her and the person to whom she is listening.

4. Unheard Ideas

To build engagement around an idea that comes from your head, you need to speak as well as listen. Engaged Listening is indeed a great way to collect opinions and needs. But you also need to verbalize your idea or proposal so that people know how to engage with you. If you remain silent, that never happens. In order to inspire others to move forward with your idea, opinion, or advice, or to bring about a change you want to see, first solicit ideas through observing the situation, asking questions, and listening to the responses. Then take the next important step: state your unique point of view and opinion and share your compelling vision. The world deserves to hear it.

Your Next Steps

Even though Engaged Listening, like other strengths, can be overused, it remains one of your most valuable Quiet Influence tools. As an introvert who naturally tends to listen instead of talk, you will significantly improve your influence when you maximize Engaged Listening to the fullest degree. Because Engaged Listening feeds the strengths of Focused Conversations, Writing, and Thoughtful Use of Social Media, it is a prime way to increase your QIQ. To get started, first consolidate what you've learned in this chapter. Here are five points to remember:

1. Observe body language and tune into voices to understand the message beneath the words.
2. To help you develop a deep understanding of the people and situations you are trying to influence, make an effort to get together face-to-face.
3. Giving others the chance to reflect and respond is a gift.
4. Engaged Listening engenders empathy, establishes credibility, and builds engagement—all of which help form the trusted relationships necessary for influence.
5. In addition to listening you also need to verbalize your idea or proposal so that people know how to engage with you.

Next, listen to yourself as you answer these questions:

1. How did someone who truly listened to you impact you? What Engaged Listening skills did the person use? How can you use similar Engaged Listening skills to influence someone else?

2. Who in your circle of influence could you listen to more to gain key knowledge or insights? Can you prepare three key questions to ask during an upcoming focused conversation?

3. How can Engaged Listening help you with the influencing challenge you listed in chapter 3? Could Engaged Listening help you develop empathy with a person involved in that situation? What could you listen for to learn more about the situation?

As important as it is, Engaged Listening is only one tool in your Quiet Influence toolbox. You need to be able to use it to understand positions, draw out people and through interaction and active dialogue move your ideas forward. That means going beyond Engaged Listening to Focused Conversations, the subject of the next chapter.

Chapter 7

Quiet Influence Strength #4: Focused Conversations

"And now whatever way our stories end I know you have re-written mine. . . . Because I knew you, I have been changed for good"

Steven Schwartz, Composer, *Wicked*

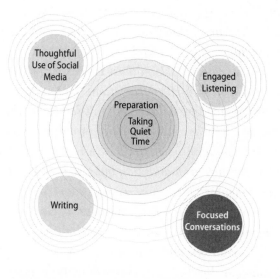

Haley Kilpatrick was an introverted fifteen-year-old in Albany, Georgia, when she was compelled to turn her frustration into action. Having felt out-of-place as a middle-school student, she wanted to help her younger sister get through those tough years with fewer challenges. Her solution: starting a

mentoring program that paired middle-school girls with high-school students who had survived and thrived.

After sharing and shaping her vision with her supportive mom, Haley approached her school principal to propose a program in which high-school girls would meet for one hour weekly with interested middle-school girls. Together, they would tackle the middle-school girls' problems. Her principal agreed. When 80 percent of the middle school's girls came to the first meeting, Haley knew she had struck a chord. "That fall day in 2002 changed everything. . . . In that moment I realized just how much these girls needed support and guidance." Girl Talk was born.

Haley grew the organization during her remaining high-school years. After Cosmo Girl magazine reported on the successful program, hundreds of letters arrived from young women wanting to bring Girl Talk to their schools. Full of energy and a belief in her cause, Haley ran the growing nonprofit while also working and earning her undergraduate degree.

As Haley reflects back on those beginnings, she sees that she relied on quiet, focused conversations to promote Girl Talk. In one such session, she influenced a full-service marketing firm to donate a website and office space. Another conversation brought in philanthropist Ron Bell, who not only provided funding through his foundation but also become a trusted business mentor. One by one, Haley's conversations resulted in many more people signing on to be part of Girl Talk's success.

The program itself is successful precisely because it revolves around one-on-one and small group discussions that provide rich dialogue. By 2012, Girl Talk was active in forty-three states and had reached more than 40,000 girls. Of those middle-school girls who have participated in the program, 83 percent have chosen to go on to become Girl Talk leaders in high school. According to Girl Talk staff, studies have also demonstrated academic improvement among participants.

Haley is very clear about her talents: "My strengths are program development, writing, research, and product development—all of which require very little people time. I am also learning that the little bit of extrovert in me is eager to shine when furthering our mission."

In an effort to extend the program's reach in a way that uses her strengths, Haley wrote The Drama Years, a book that draws on the many conversations she has had. It offers advice for navigating the tough terrain of teenage life[27] Haley looks ahead to a Girl Talk future that could potentially impact millions of middle-school girls around the world with important messages about self-esteem and self-worth.

How have you used conversations to move others forward? For introverts like Haley Kilpatrick, influence comes in the form of focused conversations with one person at a time. Haley's initial one-on-one discussions with her mom and high-school principal were just the beginning of her Quiet Influence strategy that continued to rely on face-to-face meetings. In fact, in Haley's case, the very success of the program and her book revolve around the power of focused, small-group conversation. As Doug Conant, the introverted leader and former CEO of Campbell Soup Company, pronounces, "The action is in the interaction."[28] Interpersonal interaction through focused conversations is where much of the work of influence gets done. These opportunities allow you to understand the views of others and express your own opinions so that you can influence people and situations in profound and lasting ways.

If you are especially introverted, you may be cringing already at the thought of initiating and participating in more conversations. Hang in there: it's worth it. A focused conversation is not the same as the chitchat that drives you up the wall and out the door. Instead, these are dialogues with a specific point in which you combine listening and purposeful talking. Because you've invested in Taking Quiet Time, Preparation, Engaged Listening, and perhaps Writing and Thoughtful Use of Social Media, you have set yourself up to be a capable conversationalist. Each Quiet Influence strength helps you connect with other people—through building up your energy and confidence, through being there for them, or through sharing your ideas with others. The resulting connection feeds right into an effective conversation that in turn solidifies a relationship to use for influencing. In addition, you will often gain insight through a conversation that can feed back into Preparation or spill over into your Writing and Thoughtful Use of Social Media. All in all, the strength of Focused Conversations represents a point of convergence for all of the strengths, and as such, is often a critical part of a Quiet Influencer's approach.

Focused Conversations and Influence

With Focused Conversations, once again, Quiet Influencers use their strengths to give rather than take on their way to influence. Putting Focused Conversations front and center increases your QIQ and your ability to influence. These interactions give you the opportunity to provide support and encouragement, spark learning, solve problems, and work through conflict.

1. Provide Support and Encouragement

Dale was a budding graphic designer enrolled in art school in Toronto, Canada. As the competition intensified among her talented classmates, she began having doubts about whether she should pursue the uncertain career path ahead. At a show where her work was being exhibited, Dale gathered the courage to approach José, a prominent and successful designer in town. Dale asked him to take a look at her work and provide her with an honest opinion. After spending some time looking at her drawings, he took Dale aside to talk. He told her that she was very talented and gave her specific steps to take her skill to the next level. Dale recalls, "He encouraged me not to abandon my dream." She followed José's advice and through perseverance her career blossomed. Even ten years later, Dale is extremely aware of the importance of this conversation. "Had I not had that conversation, I might have given up. His words made all the difference in my decision to keep pursuing my art."

Many people share similar stories about a teacher, boss, parent, uncle, friend, or even a random stranger who encouraged them in a focused one-on-one encounter. This kind of individualized encouragement can have a deep and lasting impact, influencing the very direction of a person's life. It is often the catalyst for provoking a new way of thinking and encouraging someone to move forward to take action.

2. Spark Learning

Gaining multiple perspectives through focused conversations also helps you to generate new ideas and clarify positions. Through give-and-take discussions, you glean information and insight that can help with the preparation and writing aspects of Quiet Influence. A conversation delivers a different kind of learning than pure listening: you can put ideas out there to test and develop in addition to absorbing the ideas and information others offer. Writer Cliff Kuong advises, "Just being around another creative person is vital to the process because so many ideas happen as a result of water-cooler chatter and passing contact."[29]

Quiet Influencers also use focused conversations to help others learn. Patrick, a plant manager in a nuclear facility, holds monthly meetings to which he invites several selected workers from each department. These low-key sessions are opportunities for people to air concerns, ask questions, and learn about new management initiatives from him and one another. The new insights that are shared between individuals in this informal manifestation of focused conversations also end up helping departments work more effectively together.

Quiet Influencers also structure more formal processes to spur learning through conversation. Sam is a well-respected manager in a fast-moving IT department. In order to stay on top of the latest changes in his area, he has created an innovative learning model based on focused conversations. He dubs it "Teach Me Something I Don't Know," and it has become a big hit. Each of his IT architects prepares a fifteen-minute presentation about a new technology, idea, or problem and delivers that presentation to Sam at a scheduled time. They discuss the topic from many angles. Both Sam and his employees report tremendous benefits from these lively sessions of mutual learning. It keeps them on their toes and Sam on top of the latest info in a rapidly changing field.

Sometimes, such learning can mean life or death. Elisha, the nurse whose story appeared at the beginning of chapter 6, uses direct, focused conversations to help parents of very ill children learn about the implications of missed appointments. Believing their children are strong, some parents resist medicine for their kids. They miss chemotherapy appointments—even though just one week of delay can lead to a child relapsing. In a focused conversation, Elisha listens to the parents' perspective and concerns. She then presents the honest picture of potential death. She is firm and direct with them about the dire consequences of missing either medicine or treatments. In many cases, she has been able, through these discussions, to influence them to do the right thing and comply with the medical recommendations.

3. Solve Problems

The writer Sophia Dembling said, "I love having a really long, deep, navel-gazing, analytical conversation. I have one girlfriend I love talking to. Anytime we go anywhere, it will be time to say good-bye and we'll sit in the parking lot for an hour finishing our conversation. We went away for a weekend once, and by the end of the weekend, I am not kidding, our jaws hurt!"

Thoughtful conversation allows you to meander down both linear and circular paths in order to explore problems from many different angles. Both the perspective gained and the opportunity to hear another person's suggestions bring solutions into focus. These solutions can often open up significant opportunities for influence because they present an alternative to the status quo and instigate the next right action.

Take an example shared by Jake, the Quiet Influencer we met at the beginning of chapter 5. He recounted this story: "Last week I outlined a staffing plan based on a brainstorming session and sent it to a colleague for feedback. Then we talked about it. I made sure to ask questions about her perspective—not just whether she agreed with something I said or even what she thought about it, but also whether she felt confident in the decisions we were arriving at, what hesitations or questions were still on her mind, and if she felt our decisions might impact her other work. She provided clear answers." Through this conversation, Jake and his colleague solved the problem of how to move forward, and Jake was able to greatly influence the next steps.

4. Work through Conflict

Quiet Influencers build on their natural tendency for deeper conversation to manage interpersonal conflict. They help others move forward by being intentional about these interactions. Barbara McFadden Allen, a nonprofit manager, describes her effective conflict resolution approach: "After a group meeting, I will often follow up with a phone call to the key decision-makers and preferably personally visit their office. I find that my thoughts are clearer, my arguments are more effective, and the opportunity to influence is more effective in that setting. And typically the individual I'm working with has surprisingly different positions or viewpoints from those they expressed (or from those I understood) in the meeting."

Focused conversations can be particularly useful to work through conflict that simmers through email. Matt Underwood is the principal of a middle school that he describes as "email-centered." To role model how to put email in its place, he consistently uses it only as a tool for distributing basic information, not for expressing his views, especially when sensitive issues are involved. Instead, he talks face to face when he has an unresolved problem. "There's just so much that can be gained by being physically near a person that being at a keyboard and behind the screen does not convey." Barbara Davis, a parent of one of Matt's students, confirmed the impact of his focused conversations. "I never felt like he was distant. There are people you can talk to who feel sterile. . . . I never felt that way with Matt. Even through email he made me feel my concerns as a parent were important."

How to Use Focused Conversations to Influence

Quiet Influencers make the most of their focused conversations by setting up spaces and times to talk, strengthening their case, and being authentic and flexible. Some Quiet Influencers shine in formal, planned conversations. Others are more comfortable in less structured environments. Some swear by face-to-face conversations, and others find the telephone just as effective. Many prefer one-on-one or small group discussions rather than large gatherings. With the tips that follow, you can increase your QIQ and get the most out of your conversations, no matter what they look like or where they take place.

1. Set Up Space and Times to Talk

Use your space   Design or use your workspace to enhance conversations when you choose to have them. Keep your space neat and inviting. If yours is the only chair that isn't full of files, you might be missing out on a chance to hold an important influencing conversation because you are not inviting people to sit and talk with you. If you work in a noisy or busy open space environment, you, like most introverts, may find it hard to focus on what someone is saying. Suggest the conversation be moved to a conference room or outdoors for a walk. When you know in advance that you want to engage, schedule a conference room.

Make time for face time In order to build relationships and influence others, Joyce Ramsey-Coleman, chief nursing officer at Children's Health Care of Atlanta, makes a special effort to carve out face time with her nurses. "I try to remember what I know about a person and build from that or I ask about a specific patient or a general nursing question."[30]

John Maeda, the introverted head of the Rhode Island School of Design, learned that his multiple daily tweets and "cyber style leadership" were not the right approach. He rebounded from an 80 percent no-confidence vote from the faculty by getting out from behind his computer and spending time meeting with individuals. "He followed a piece of advice from his pal John Jay, Wieden+Kennedy's executive creative director," reported *Fast Company* magazine. "Posted on Maeda's office wall is Jay's '10 Lessons for Young Designers.' No. 2 on the list: Life is visceral. Get off the computer and connect with real people."[31]

Allow for serendipity Let your inspiration come from walking around and be open to the ideas that emerge from chance conversations. Casual conversations can lead to creative breakthroughs and conflict resolution, so, like John Maeda learned, don't hole up in your office all of the time. Selah Abrams, an engineer you will learn more about in chapter 9, shares his insight about the power of chance meetings in this way: "My family is from New Orleans and the world comes to us, so we naturally love to watch people and learn from them, seeing how we're the same and how we are different—you can read people like a good book, and if you engage them in conversation, you can learn even more. . . ."

WHEN FACE TO FACE ISN'T POSSIBLE

Chances are, you work with people at a distance. Sometimes, face-to-face focused conversations are not possible. More and more work is being done through teleconference or video conference technology. You can still excel at these conversations and incorporate them into your influencing approach. Use these tips to make the most of "virtual" meetings.

1. Become familiar with the technology. Don't miss your opportunity to influence because you are preoccupied with troubleshooting technology. Work through technical issues before the meeting.

2. Be sensitive to time zone differences. If you're in charge of scheduling a virtual meeting, don't plan meetings too early or too late for others. You're likely to end up with tired or rushed people who aren't at their best for a productive conversation.

3. Plan questions for group input. A virtual conversation needs even more guidance than a face-to-face conversation. Prepare open-ended questions so that you are sure to hear from everyone involved. Great questions can spark enlightening conversations.

4. Take advantage of video. Although not exactly face-to-face, video technologies do let you see the facial expressions of others in the meeting. You'll be able to pick up on those clues that can transform basic information sharing into an effective interpersonal conversation.

5. Utilize chats and polls. Chats and polls invite people to participate in a way that generates the give-and-take associated with a conversation. Plus, these features keep people engaged and awake.

6. Tag team with a "producer." Reduce your stress and increase your ability to participate in the conversation by delegating the technology aspects to someone else just as you would ask someone else to facilitate a live meeting.

2. Strengthen Your Case

Wait to speak   Take your time to listen and observe what is going on. Doing so can make your comments land with more impact. Find ways to ease into an active role in the interaction. Introvert Wesley Hopkins, RN, manages a cardiovascular unit. He explains, "It takes a moment for me to warm up and be a free communicator, but this extra time helps me to be a patient observer and not jump to errant conclusions." In group settings, Ronnie Wilkins, a nonprofit executive, purposely refrains from speaking or dominating the discussion. After his initial silence, if he thinks the group is missing an important point, he then contributes. When he does, others are more likely to listen because his voice has not been dominating the room. Victoria, an introverted marketing manager, has a similar approach. She imagines herself as the great blue heron that swoops in when she has something important to say as opposed to one of many cackling geese that keep squawking away.

Use Repetition   You may need to repeat a message multiple times in order to get it to stick. Jody Wirtz, the banking professional we first met in chapter 2, says, "As a source of influence, repetition is the key. . . . If I have two or three key thoughts or concepts, I will continually work those into conversations until I feel as if they have sunk in."

Float your arguments   Use focused conversations to bounce ideas off of people as you craft and shape your arguments in the preparation stage of influence. Finance professional Kristin said that she offered an idea to shift responsibilities from one manager to another. "I had a convincing argument that was well thought out," she remembers. "Discussing it one on one with several of my colleagues and gaining their individual support was more effective than discussing it in front of the entire group at once."

3. Be Authentic and Flexible

Tell stories   Prepare stories and examples to make conversations come alive and bring the person or people you're speaking with

AEIOU: MORE THAN JUST A BUNCH OF VOWELS

As easy to remember as the alphabet, the AEIOU communication tool helps keep you on course during important conversations. This model helps ensure that the person you are speaking with not only understands your points but also collaborates with you on a win-win solution. Use it before a discussion in order to plan your approach so that the other person gets what you are saying and the conversation ends with a tangible future action that can be the first step in influencing others to move forward. **AEIOU** helps you remember these important steps:

Acknowledge the other person's positive intentions.

Express your thoughts and feelings.

Identify your proposal.

Outline the benefits of the outcome.

Understand each other and check.

Let's say that you want to influence a colleague in another department to move forward more quickly on an important project like a new website that features content from his group. Here's how you might use **AEIOU** to move the action forward:

Acknowledge: "I know we both want this website to be a success."

Express: "I realize you are on deadline with the Jupiter project and that you've been busy, but I am concerned your department has missed the deadline for the website content. This will put us behind our agreed-upon launch date and set back the marketing program."

Identify: "I propose that our intern interview your management team using a set of structured questions you have approved to gather the content we need."

Outcome: "I anticipate the content you and your team provide in these interviews will be easily reshaped for use on the website and we will be able to go forward to launch on schedule."

Understanding: "I understand we've agreed to begin these interviews next week. Thank you for your cooperation."

into the moment. Compelling stories strengthen the impact of your case because the ones you choose to share say as much about you as they do about the subject. Haley Kilpatrick told a story from a visit she made to a Girl Talk summer camp. "A reserved young girl who was consistently made fun of at school sat down at the lunch table. I watched as three girls introduced themselves and sat down next to her. By the end of the week, this shy girl was in the midst of all the fun—singing, dancing, and opening up about her experiences. She is now giving back as a counselor. It was great to witness how in just one week, Girl Talk helped build her self-esteem and show her that she is perfect just the way she is." When Haley weaves stories like this into her conversations, she demonstrates the influence of her program in a very visceral manner.

Tune into others to determine when to talk   Pick up on others' "vibes" by observing their body language and listening to their words. Decide if they feel like talking or not; you will not be an effective influencer if you force a conversation on someone who is not in the mood to converse. Jason, an introverted lawyer, appreciates the administrative professional in his eighteen-person department for her ability to read people's moods. Using this insight, she knows when—and when not to—talk. If you do decide to pursue a conversation, show people that you are tuning in by lowering or raising your voice to match the other person's state of mind.

Use the same techniques to adjust your conversations with people you've not met before. Sam Horn, an author and "intrigue expert" has developed a particularly effective visual for assessing how your idea or content is being received. She calls it the "the eyebrow test." Sam says, "Explain your idea, proposal, or request to the other person . . . using the exact same sixty-second opening you'll use in the meeting. Then, watch her eyebrows. If her eyebrows are knit or furrowed, she's puzzled. She didn't get it. And if *she* didn't get it, *you* won't get it. Why? Because confused people don't ask for clarification, and they don't say yes to your idea. You want their eyebrows to go UP. That means they're intrigued. They want to know more. That means you just got your idea or request in their mental door. If what you're pitching gets their eyebrows up, good for you. That means, 'Game's on.' If it doesn't, back to the drawing board."[32]

Offer up information about yourself   Share information about yourself so that the other person understands you better. Although talking about yourself may be uncomfortable, it will be worth it because you will be more likely to build the kind of connection that's important to influence. The one-on-one or small-group scenario provides a safe backdrop for sharing, even if you tend to value privacy. Remember that not everyone will understand your hesitancy to share. Take the initiative to tell people why you aren't always an open book. Girl Talk's Haley Kilpatrick, for instance, is open with her staff about her introversion. "I have learned the importance of telling the people I work closely with that I am an introvert and explaining what that means. It helps them to better understand how I recharge and also helps me balance the amount of people time required for Girl Talk."

Overuse of Focused Conversations

It's hard to imagine how meaningful conversations could negatively impact your ability to influence. But if you ask introverts, most will tell you that too much of this type of communication can be utterly exhausting. Overuse of Focused Conversations can result in an invasion of privacy, confounded problems, group think, and the limitation of words.

1. Invasion of Privacy

The sharing of private or personal information that is sometimes expected in conversations can be especially troubling for introverts. You don't want others to push you in this way, so watch that you don't step into that space yourself. People won't listen

---

HOW TO INITIATE CONVERSATIONS

If you are like most introverts, the hardest part of a focused conversation is getting it going. That task is easier if you are the chair of a meeting or if you preplan a conversation on a specific topic. In those cases, you can simply jump into a prepared agenda. But what if the conversation is in an informal setting? How can you start it off in a way that helps ensure it won't slip into the kind of personal small talk you hate and that is unlikely directly further your influencing goals? The answer is stepping into conversations with substance-filled questions like the following.

Conversation Kick-off Questions to Use at Internal Events

What project have you been working on?
What is most interesting about your current work?
What is a change going on right now in your area? How is it going?
What have you learned from working in your area?
What brought you to this company?

Conversation Kick-off Questions to Use at External Events Such as Conferences

What brought you to this meeting?
What do you know about the speaker?
What interests you about this session?
What is the best new idea you have heard so far?

---

to you if they feel you are coming on too strong either emotionally or physically. In role-plays of networking conversations, one can see introverts literally backing away as more aggressive types move into their physical proximity. Likewise, incessant questions—even those posed in the spirit of support—can shut down dialogue. Many introverts respond to a barrage of questions with reactions like this: "I feel like I am on the witness stand. I can't wait for the cross-examination to end."

2. Confounded Problems

Talking through potential solutions in a Focused Conversation certainly can lead to great influencing results. However, you need to balance conversing with the opportunity to observe from the outside, review other significant inputs and data. The answer to a problem does not always come forth through interaction. Sometimes interaction can confuse situations and compound rather than solve problems.

Take this example of how one hotel staff should have conducted research rather than try to solve a problem through conversation. Nikhil, a frequent traveler, had no choice but to climb down twenty flights of stairs when the elevator in his hotel was out of service. He was under pressure to be on time for an appointment, and this situation caused him stress and discomfort. The next day during checkout, Nikhil requested an adjustment to his bill to compensate for the situation. The front desk staff person, who had not been on duty the previous day, peppered him with questions instead of researching the situation. Nikhil felt interrogated and unheard. He did not feel that the staff resolved the situation, and ultimately he decided not to return to the hotel even though it was in a convenient location for his ongoing business.

3. Group Think

Solving problems in a group can be frustrating at best—especially when well-meaning colleagues bring out the brainstorming option. Organizations often use brainstorming to generate ideas. If not well facilitated, however, brainstorming becomes a chance for the talkers to dominate and promote their ideas. Introverts who are reticent to speak up or need some time to tap into their reserve of ideas find little chance to contribute. The result: the loudest person's point of view takes on artificial significance. Other people are pulled into the wake of this idea, and other points of view fall into the shadows. The result is a lopsided solution that is not reflective of all of the power in the room. Because such free-for-all brainstorming has become so common, this trend has been called the rise of *Group Think*. If you are not the one talking, your opportunity for influence diminishes. You would do better to try to steer the group away from the brainstorming "conversation" and toward a more balanced way at arriving at a solution.

4. The Limitations of Words

Sometimes words can fail you, and it is better to keep your mouth shut. In other chapters we have looked at the power of silence and writing down one's thoughts before speaking. When wrestling with a conflict, trying to talk things out too much or explaining yourself repeatedly can be counterproductive and leave both parties talking in circles. People need time to absorb difficult news and often require time to be alone in order to process a difficult discussion. Too much conversation at these times can actually inflame a conflict.

Meg, a hospital social worker, coordinates services for the elderly. She received an angry phone call from an adult daughter of one of her patients. This daughter blamed Meg for going behind her back in arranging a rehabilitation placement for her mom. The fact was that Meg had tried to reach the daughter numerous times and did not receive a return phone call. She and the mom had reached a solution without the daughter's input. Meg knew that this woman's aggressive behavior was most likely driven by anxiety and concern and that any response she made would likely increase the tension. So she wisely kept her lips sealed to avoid inflaming an already stressful situation. When the daughter calmed down, she was able to plan for the next needed steps.

Your Next Steps

Focused Conversations, especially those you conduct face to face, represent the nexus of Quiet Influence. They build from the energy you generate from Taking Quiet Time, contribute to your

Preparation, give you an unequaled opportunity for Engaged Listening, and inform your Writing and Thoughtful Use of Social Media. In addition, Focused Conversations work for both introverts and extroverts. When you initiate a conversation with extroverts, you'll give them the chance they need to think out loud. As an introvert, you'll appreciate that you can engage with people at a deeper level. Rest assured that this is a conversation strategy that will contribute to your ability to make a difference, challenge the status quo, and help others move forward.

To hone your ability to make the most of your Focused Conversations strength, begin by considering these five key points from the chapter:

1. Influence frequently comes in the form of Focused Conversations, often one person at a time.

2. Prepare questions ahead of time for more productive conversations.

3. Carve out opportunities for random encounters in your workplace.

4. After listening carefully, swoop in like a blue heron with one question or observation that commands attention.

5. Conversations can be exhausting. When you see that your energy is depleted, take a break.

Next, step away from conversations to consider these questions:

1. Reflect on a Focused Conversation with a manager or co-worker that moved you forward. How did the conversation help bring a solution into focus? What can you learn from that experience that you can take to other Focused Conversations?

2. What is the next type of email you could replace with a Focused Conversation, either in person or over the phone? If so, how will you initiate the conversation and what questions will you ask?

3. How you can learn from others in your next dialogue? Also think of a pivotal story or anecdote you can share to illustrate a central point related to your influencing challenge. How can you weave that into your next conversation to see how it plays?

If the chapters on Engaged Listening and Focused Conversations have pushed you out of your office and your comfort zone, don't get discouraged. It gets easier with practice. Yes, although a lot of influence happens in the moment with people, much emerges through Writing, the next Quiet Influence strength we will explore.

Chapter 8

Quiet Influence Strength #5: Writing

"Writing, to me, is simply thinking through my fingers."

Isaac Asimov, Author

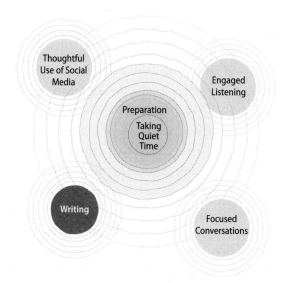

As an introvert, Helen Thorpe strongly preferred staying in the background in her role as political wife to Colorado governor John Hickenlooper. As an accomplished journalist, though, she rarely shies away from tackling politically sensitive and complicated social issues. Her first nonfiction book, Just Like Us: The

True Story of Four Mexican Girls Coming of Age in America,[33] *has received critical praise and is a riveting piece of journalism.*

In preparation to writing the book, Thorpe spent five years following the journey of four teenage Mexican girls through high school and then college in Denver, Colorado. Two of the girls were from families who were in the United States legally and two had parents who had entered illegally. Thorpe takes readers along through the twists and turns of these girls' lives. Through their personal dramas, she powerfully enters the debate about immigration.

"This is not a policy book," she explained. "You understand the policy debate by reading about the human story. You really get what it means to be legal or illegal." In speaking about the book, Thorpe described a girl named Marisela. "She is so eloquent and can speak so much to her parents' situation and hers. It is not a situation with any easy answers, but she manages to articulate why it is painful to be who she is. . . . I have compassion for their traumatic experience. There is no way for them to get a green card."

Helen Thorpe definitely knows that the questions around immigration have no easy answers. Through her writing, she has gained a deep appreciation for the complexity of an issue that has economic, social justice, and deeply human components. Thorpe knows that through her writing she can challenge the status quo by provoking new thinking and deepening public awareness. Her words have indeed moved her readers. One reviewer illustrated the influential power of Thorpe's prose through this comment: "Thorpe raises pressing philosophical questions about the immigration debate throughout the book, engaging and challenging the reader to decide for him- or herself what to think. The writer doesn't let her readers off the hook. I don't believe the book was intended to be a work of advocacy journalism, but it turned out that way. You simply cannot care about actual human beings and be against progressive, humane immigration reform."[34]

Are you able to connect others to your ideas and challenge the status quo through your writing? Do you seek to inspire others by using the written word? Helen Thorpe's writing served the very important and inspiring purpose of connecting readers to the characters in her narrative. This connection widens the readers' perspective, encourages them to feel compassion, and involves them in the national discussion of this emotionally laden issue. Generating that kind of engagement is what influence is about.

Certainly, writers like Helen Thorpe challenge conventional wisdom, effect change, and help others to move forward to take action. Because introverts tend to prefer writing to talking, they often tap into writing as a powerful influencing strength. On the job, they opt for email over the telephone and are likely to prefer writing reports to making presentations. Writing offers them time to process and think. Sitting still in this seemingly solitary pursuit, alone but for their thoughts and their pen or keyboard, they relax in their comfort zone. From this confidence-building base, Quiet Influencers also write to forge very deep interpersonal connections. When done well, the process of writing develops a depth of thinking and authenticity that jump off the page and can deeply influence others.

Whether communicating tricky positions, outlining arguments, eliciting compassion, or sharing intense feelings, the written word stands as a potent mode of expression. Even though the form writing takes today is shorter, clearer, and more to the point than in the past, readers can become involved by underlining, highlighting, and thinking about the intended message in these pieces; they come to really understand what is being said. In the case of correspondence, they can be part of the dialogue by replying back with a thoughtful response.

Writing is one of the Quiet Influence strengths that transfer messages from inside your head to the outside world where they can really make a difference. Because Quiet Influencers generally invest in Taking Quiet Time and Preparation before beginning to write, they tend to put forth arguments and positions that really get through to others. When mixed with Engaged Listening, Focused Conversations, and a Thoughtful Use of Social Media, Writing can amp up your influence. And, as this chapter will show, delivering the gift of well-expressed written thoughts can even change lives.

If your QIQ is lower than you would like—and especially if you are challenged by the three strengths that take your ideas out into the world (Engaged Listening, Focused Conversations, and Thoughtful Use of Social Media), consider beginning your developmental journey with Writing. Writing feeds Thoughtful Use of Social Media; they both rely on the same fundamentals of making an impact through words. By starting here, you can shore up a very powerful avenue of influence.

Writing and Influence

Writing can contribute to your ability to influence in four ways: by clarifying your own stance, advocating your position, connecting with others, and motivating others to action.

1. Clarify Your Own Stance

You become clear and purposeful in your influencing efforts only after you gain awareness of your own true stance on an issue. As anyone who keeps a journal knows, writing helps you to gain clarity about what's important to you and what you think and feel about situations. When you put pen to paper, or fingers to the keyboard, the words often flow as if they are writing themselves. You're able to release and better understand strong emotions such as anger and resentment—feelings that may cloud the clarity of thinking you need to influence others. You can then merge your passionate feelings with logic and clarity to form a well constructed case.

Free writing is a term used to describe an unfiltered writing exercise done in a set time period. In his book *Accidental Genius*, which focuses on this method as a breakthrough strategy, Author Mark Levy suggests, "Free writing encourages you to think more honestly and resourcefully than before. You are then able to generate breakthrough ideas and solutions that you couldn't have created any other way. . . . It pushes the brain to think longer, harder, deeper, and more unconventionally than it normally would."[35]

Writing also provides you with the opportunity to think through and refine your plan. Jessica Handler, an author and writing instructor, suggests you engage in a free write before constructing professional correspondence. Prior to beginning, ask yourself, "What do you want this email to accomplish? Do you want to be friends with this person, do you want to calm them down, do you want to get them involved in a project and why?"[36]

2. Advocate a Position

Once they have used writing exercises to figure out where they stand on an issue, Quiet Influencers continue to use the written word to sell others on their position. They often are more comfortable advocating for their proposal in writing as opposed to in person. Plus, they tend to be very persuasive on the page. Their clear writing helps others move from a state of confusion to a fuller understanding of a situation. Introvert Ronnie Wilkins, a nonprofit manager, believes he is more effective when he writes clearly and coherently than when he tries to speak persuasively. Case in point: a survey of his membership about potential meeting sites revealed that people hadn't understood the rationale he had previously outlined verbally. Ronnie decided to write an article in the organization's newsletter. In that piece, he was able to clearly articulate a persuasive case that did the trick. Afterward, members told him they better understood the issues and felt satisfied with the rationale he had provided. After that, the meeting organizing team made a site decision quickly.

Ashley, top sales professional at an insurance sales company, uses writing to subtly advocate for her company's reputation as an industry leader. She writes to share important market trends that may cause her clients problems in the future. Ashley believes that her company's strong track record of sales is largely due to consistently providing these written reports. Through these pieces, she positions her company as the most knowledgeable partner for her clients. The information she provides helps them minimize their risks—and that's a critical success factor for insurance firms. This approach influences them to sign on the dotted line. Ashley says, "It's a marathon, not a sprint, and we build up credibility with our prospects. . . . When we write these reports effectively, the sale happens."

3. Connect with Others

Quiet Influencers understand that influence never happens in a vacuum. Even though solitary quiet time can be a great preparation for influence, influence most often involves encouraging others to think or act in a different manner. For that reason, interpersonal connection lies at the heart of influence: if you don't relate to others in some way, it's unlikely you will influence them.

Writing provides an attractive and powerful alternative for connecting with people, whether one-on-one or in groups. Introverts are often more comfortable using writing than speaking in person to address conflict or convey messages to large groups. Author Sophia Dembling remembers that when she was having a problem with a friend, she would write her a letter instead of talking to her about her feelings. Through writing, she was able to fully express herself, and her candor allowed them to then discuss what they needed to address and move on.

Like the pen pals of old, people today write emails and engage in social media sites to enter and maintain deep relationships. When you clearly express your thoughts and feelings, your

WRITING CAN CAUSE A STIR

"Today is my last day at Goldman Sachs. After almost twelve years at the firm—first as a summer intern while at Stanford, then in New York for ten years, and now in London—I believe I have worked here long enough to understand the trajectory of its culture, its people, and its identity. And I can honestly say that the environment now is as toxic and destructive as I have ever seen it. . . .

"I hope this can be a wake-up call to the board of directors. Make the client the focal point of your business again. Without clients you will not make money. In fact, you will not exist. Weed out the morally bankrupt people; no matter how much money they make for the firm. And get the culture right again, so people want to work here for the right reasons. People who care only about making money will not sustain this firm—or the trust of its clients—for very much longer."[37]

In a shot heard around editorial pages of leading newspapers, Greg Smith resigned from his position as a Goldman Sachs executive director and head of the firm's US equity derivatives business in Europe, the Middle East, and Africa. He caused the stir by simultaneously issuing his written resignation statement to both his company and to the media.

Although you may not agree with the approach that Mr. Smith used, you can't deny that this one resignation letter clearly challenged the status quo about how employees everywhere handle negative views of their firms. Whether any change occurs as a result of this letter remains to be seen. It certainly did receive a lot of attention and elicit responses from the firm and from thousands of newspaper readers. Plus, this one written document of a mere 1,270 words provoked countless water cooler conversations and online dialogues.

Greg Smith's writing and influencing days have continued. Shortly after his public resignation, he landed a $1.5 million advance on a book deal.

readers can thoughtfully consider what you say and gain a connection with you in ways that may not be possible through regular conversation.

Executive Coach Vinay Kumar believes that the genesis for his coaching role with clients emerged from his writing for professional forums. People read his postings and valued his expertise. They then asked him to be on committees, write papers, and speak at professional conferences. "If I had to go out or and make phone calls to make connections, I wouldn't have done it. I find that very draining." Yet through his writing, Vinay makes connections, gains referrals, and inspires entrepreneurs, coaches, and salespeople to take risks. He receives constant feedback through writing that he is making a big difference in their lives.

4. Motivate Others to Action

Writing can inspire others to act, and it can do so with very few words. Julie, the administrative professional introduced in chapter 4, created posters about her blind-spot safety program and placed them around her work area. "In my posters and presentations, the emotional overtones are tremendous," she said. She positioned questions like, "Have you checked your blind spot lately?" above photos of young children standing behind vehicles. Julie reflects, "Parents were drawn to the displays and wanted to know more about what we were doing." Many did as Julie had suggested and tried out the test at home with their kids and pets. They talked to neighbors, friends, family member, and co-workers about the power of the backing-up experiment. It's easy to see how accidents could have been avoided because of Julie's printed questions and proactive steps.

Josh, the operations manager, sends positive emails of encouragement to individuals. Other Quiet Influencers, like Doug Conant, are known for taking the time to send handwritten notes. Touched by the attention, individuals will often hold onto these symbols of recognition for years. Writing makes it official. Some recipients have told Josh that glancing at these little confidence boosters helped them get through some rough days at work. The permanence of the written word means that these mementos can motivate people to action again and again and in a variety of situations.

How to Write for Influence

Quiet Influencers transform their innate writing skills into a powerful influencing strength by knowing and adapting to the audience, attending to the craft of writing, and making a persuasive case.

1. Know and Adapt to the Audience

Practice WIIFM Remember WIIFM when you're trying to put together a persuasive appeal. WIIFM stands for "What's in it for me?" and the "me" refers to the person you are trying to influence. Why should he or she care about what you're writing? What's his or her self-interest? One trick that can help you come up with the most insightful answers to these questions is taking the time to "sit in someone else's chair." Take for example writing a proposal to your boss. Imagine yourself in her chair before you begin drafting your proposal. Ask yourself if she is driven by saving money. (What boss isn't?) Is she propelled by new, cutting-edge ideas? Is she focused on the customer as a priority? Is she mainly worried about looking good to her bosses? Position your written case with these motivators in mind, and you will have a much higher chance of scoring success.

Pay attention to tone Follow speaker and author Dr. Tony Alessandra's "platinum rule": "Do unto others as they would like to be done unto."[38] Flex to the other person's style. Sending emails with personal niceties and questions like "How was your weekend?" can work for some people but are a turn-off to others who want to go right to the task at hand. Some people prefer high-level bullet points whereas others want more a more detailed, specific explanation. Notice the style that writers use and mirror aspects of that back to them when you can. They won't consciously realize you are adapting to their style, but you will inevitably reduce the "static" when you use this tip to connect through writing.

Consider this example. Jason, a lawyer in a software company in the Midwest, reached out to his communications department. He needed to learn how to quickly get the attention of his chief financial officer and gain funding for a new position in his department. Jason was advised to streamline his memo and focus on the "numbers" instead of the words. He listened to this advice and adjusted his style. Mission accomplished! Jason gained the desired nod for his request. As a lawyer, his natural tendency would have been to explain each point methodically and completely in prose. The switch in his writing style and format contributed greatly to his influencing success.

Create thinking space for others   Use written documents to give people (especially other introverts) a chance to mull your ideas over before you initiate a conversation. Send out meeting materials well in advance of the scheduled time. Write a carefully constructed report and share it before sitting down in one-on-one conversations. Put email in its most effective place by using "the sandwich technique": write an email providing all the necessary background for a discussion. Then have the conversation in person or over the phone. Later, summarize the key points in an email that the other person can reflect upon before committing to action.

2. Attend to the Craft of Writing

Focus on depth over breadth   Introverts' writing often reveals carefully considered feelings and opinions. Take the time to construct your written piece so that the depth of your concerns and knowledge emerges clearly for the reader. Attention to depth can make the difference between a reader taking notice of your ideas or not. You may find it easier to develop that depth in writing than in person. A *Newsweek* reporter interviewed Marian Goodman, one of the world's most successful art dealers, and commented on her introverted communication style. "[She chooses] her words even more carefully than usual—a 30-second pause is normal for her—and then she expands on her answers in emails."[39] Goodman uses a classic introvert technique: speak few words, and then develop the thought process in writing.

Pay attention to the details.   Use good grammar, spelling, and punctuation. You simply cannot ignore the fundamentals of language if you are trying to influence others through your writing. Jessica Handler explains, "Grammar and spelling are part of your presentation. It is the same way you would not go to work in mismatched or inappropriate clothing."[40] She suggests having someone else check your document. "Ask a colleague to address these questions: How coherent are you? Are you repeating yourself? Are you using the right tone? Are you dressed appropriately for the occasion? . . . Excellent communication," Jessica says, "will make you stand out from the crowd."

Jessica goes on to say that typos can mean the difference between being heard or discounted—between being a successful influencer and "just noise in the background." Jessica suggests paying close attention even to emails. Write an important email, place it in a "drafts" folder, and take a look at it the next morning.[41] Editor Randy Peterson calls his similar process "benign neglect." He puts a writing project aside for twenty-four to forty-eight hours and then returns to it.

Ann, the paralegal, also advises carefully reviewing your work. She spends a good part of her day writing memos and briefs. "I find that I save a lot of drafts and then go back in thirty minutes, an hour, sometimes even the next day," she explains. "If I am really trying to appeal to a group, I come in the next morning, read it over, and think 'I need this to sound friendlier' or 'I need this to sound less like legal speak than 'business speak.'" Ann does a lot of editing and rewriting because she wants her clients to know she is there to help them, not be their adversary. She inspires them to move forward by first communicating with them in terms they understand.

Use creative features to support your writing Add a variety of elements to straight paragraphs of writing. Include reflection questions. Use bullet points and other graphic elements that provide clarity or interest. To boost your writing influence with a broader audience that might not spend time on plain-Jane text, combine pictures with words. Remember that a picture can be worth a thousand words. Photos, animation, and videos are fantastic ways to bring home key points. Sunni Brown, who founded a company called Brightspot I.D., says, "Visual language is one of your best friends, and it makes an idea come to fruition." Her company combines words with doodles to ignite multiple learning modalities. These engaging moving videos replace traditional handouts.[42]

3. Make a Persuasive Case

Follow a logical sequence Use step-by-step logic to make your case. Effective Quiet Influencers are masters at this persuasive writing technique because it's a carefully thought out exposition. For example, Ashley, the insurance sales professional mentioned earlier, reveals that her sales proposals include three key elements:

1. Understanding of the client's operation

2. Aspects of her company's offering that will help the client conduct its business

3. A price quote that demonstrates how their firm will help the client grow its business, reduce its expenses, or increase its margin

Provide backup Incorporate numbers, pertinent details, and data points to convince others of your argument. Pull from the research you undertook in the Preparation stage, and then decide which facts to include by going back to the WIIFM question: provide the backup that will be most appealing to your audience. Sometimes, just one data point—when it's the right one—will persuade others. However, in most situations, especially those when the stakes are high or when you are asking for a significant change or investment, paint a picture using a variety of facts.

Be succinct   Keep it short and make it effective. You often do a better job influencing others with succinct, to-the-point writing rather than lengthy tomes. Ryan Jenkins, a sales professional and speaker on Millennials, surmises that brief, concise communication goes a long way in reaching the age cohort he knows best. This generation, he explains, has grown up with the short form of Twitter-style communication (140 characters) and text messages. But young people are not the only ones who tune out when reading long communications. "If material is not on point," he continues, "people will move onto something else and you will lose your opportunity." You can also help people focus on the main points from the beginning by providing a short executive summary at the beginning of a report. A succinct introduction teases readers and convinces them to read on.

Overuse of Writing

If you are comfortable writing, you may become stuck in a rut and overuse this Quiet Influence strength at the expense of others. Overuse of Writing can result in imprisoned ideas, inefficient communication, unexpected consequences, and loss of personal connection.

1. Imprisoned Ideas

You can miss the point of influencing others when you write so much for yourself in order to discover what you think that you get

ETHOS, LOGOS, AND PATHOS IN PERSUASIVE WRITING

When you want to convince others to take action or change their minds, craft your writing to combine three time-tested and complementary types of appeals.

Ethos: Credibility—Greek for "character"

You make your claims more believable when you develop your credibility. Defined by Aristotle, this technique is called an appeal to ethos. If you are already known to and respected by your audience, you can use the reputation of your character to appeal to ethos. If not, you can develop credibility as a trustworthy source by writing in an authoritative tone that respects differing views.

Logos: Logic—Greek for "word"

You appeal to logos by writing with clarity (an important element of style) and eliminating contradictions within the text itself. Avoid other errors in syntax and mechanics as well as factual errors in the subject matter that interfere with logic. Provide effective supporting evidence and emphasize logical reasoning.

Pathos: Emotion—Greek for "suffering" or "experience"

Although often associated with emotional appeal, pathos more specifically appeals to readers' sympathies or imagination to such an extent that they can not only identify with the writer but also have empathy with him or her. Often developed through storytelling that incorporates imagination-inspiring imagery, pathos brings the abstractions of logos into the here and now. The writer's values and beliefs become fully present, often in emotionally powerful ways that move readers to action or decision.[43]

lost in your own words. So many doctoral students across hundreds of disciplines get stuck in the thesis writing step that there's even a name for this phenomenon: the "ABD" syndrome, for "All but dissertation." Because they have typically spent years writing all kinds of research papers and taking notes, they freeze when it comes time to write the most important paper of their educational career. Why? All of the writing they have done goes in circles, and they are unable to narrow down their ideas, keep moving toward a goal, and produce a tangible document. With this lost focus and no clear goal, the more they write, the less useful it becomes. Unfortunately, the newly tested theories, scientific breakthroughs, unique perspectives on historical figures, and countless other potential contributions from these scholars never see the light of day. They remain locked inside a very educated brain or imprisoned within paper or electronic files, inaccessible to others.

To save your ideas from this fate, write enough to be prepared to share your message. Don't write so much that you're tired, bored, or confused by your own thoughts. When you find yourself circling around the same topics, switch gears to communicate with others instead of with yourself. Or better yet, take a break!

2. Inefficient Communications

Sometimes, a quick phone call or short in-person discussion works far better to motivate others than written communications. Emails—and even memos or text messages—are great tools for getting people and projects to move forward, but they can also make a muddle of things and lead to terrible inefficiency. For example, in trying to set up an event, Marcela, a board member at a children's museum, called a performer to learn more about her audio needs. This performer's outgoing message said that she didn't accept phone calls and preferred emails. Marcela complied with her request, but the ensuing electronic back and forth left Marcela in a lurch. She wanted to have a dialogue about how the performer's needs could be met within the museum's budget constraints. She felt that they would have quickly reached a workable compromise had they been able to talk through the options. The performer felt frustrated that the museum was being difficult, and she began to lose her motivation to do the job. When

Marcela and the performer finally connected by phone, they sorted it through, but due to this inefficient process, the friction lingered all the way through the event.

3. Unexpected Consequences

Sometimes jumping right to the written word when advocating your position can have serious negative career consequences. Be sure to check out your assumptions and talk to key people before hastily writing out and sharing your position in what becomes a permanent format. Lars learned this lesson the hard way. He worked in a mid-level position in a marketing organization going through a merger. Because he had some strong beliefs about upcoming departmental changes, he fired off an emotionally laden email and copied all of his direct reports. Unfortunately, he did this before talking with his boss and colleagues. The email caused major earthquakes throughout the company, and Lars was consequently demoted. In this case, advocating his position in writing made him appear impulsive, aggressive, and lacking in judgment. His career at the firm never did recover.

The issue is that putting your opinions in writing makes them "official" without the benefit of input from others. In addition, a detailed plan that advocates your proposal doesn't always account for the unexpected that occurs down the line—especially when you fail to have verbal check-ins and feedback as the project evolves. Like Lars, Alan learned this lesson the hard way. A residential interior designer, he met with his client, Cynthia, about her home renovation needs. He followed up with a long proposal that included beautiful sketches and detailed cost projections for purchases. After Cynthia approved the proposal, Alan never followed up to confirm her understanding of the terms. Furniture costs changed and the bills skyrocketed. Large invoices arrived, and Cynthia was confused and resentful that the changes were never explained. She terminated Alan's services midway through the project, and the project ended on a very sour note.

4. Loss of Personal Connection

You lose the personal touch and create frustration when you depend on writing as your sole means of communication. Though many people develop strong personal and working relationships online, these virtual connections can never fully replace voice-to-voice and face-to-face conversations that build lasting and multidimensional relationships.

I consulted with a global team based in Europe who hit the wall due to the huge quantity of emails that were flying around. Even though it felt as if there was a lot of communication, members were not in synch on major goals. One person suggested they consider videoconferencing their meetings. Introducing the team members to one another and putting a face with a name drastically improved understanding, led to goal clarification, and resulted in a reduction in the perceived need for long email chains.

In truth, email is rarely the most appropriate medium for solving problems or delivering bad news because it lacks personal connection. Josh, the operations manager, avoids giving bad news electronically. He says, "If I have to give feedback on something someone messed up on, I give it face to face or at least over the phone. Otherwise, the entire message is lost and the person can really be offended, when that was never my intention."

Your Next Steps

Quiet Influencers tend to be skillful writers and use all kinds of writing—memos, reports, publications, letters, emails—to motivate others, advocate their positions and connect with audiences. Content to sit alone perfecting this craft, they often become known and appreciated for their writing skills. If writing is an influencing strength you normally rely on, continue to develop your style and strive to be even more inspiring through words. If you don't often pursue the writing medium, give it a try. Like a muscle, the more you use it, the stronger it gets. Begin your training by reviewing these five main points from the chapter:

1. Writing can challenge your thinking and that of others because it offers depth and authenticity that jumps off the page.

2. Presenting your ideas in writing gives you time to really think through what you want to say and gives your audience time to mull over your thoughts.

3. Writing can help you connect with others—especially when you write for your reader. Use WIIFM as your guide

4. For maximum impact, hone your craft. Don't let your audience be distracted by grammar, spelling, or punctuation mistakes and use both logic and emotion to make your case.

5. Balance writing with conversations. Be especially careful not to overuse email.

Next, take some time to reflect on the following questions.

1. Identify a piece of writing that has either challenged your thinking or inspired you in the last month. Which aspects of that piece can you incorporate into your own writing?

2. What opportunities exist at work or home to refine your writing skills? Who do you know who could help you improve your writing?

3. How can you use an approach like free writing to gain clarity about how you think or feel about the influencing challenge you identified in chapter 3?

Timeless in its power, writing has been a tool of influence for thousands of years. Today, a Quiet Influencer with a great idea can go worldwide by sharing writing through a Thoughtful Use of Social Media, the next Quiet Influence Strength, which I'll cover in chapter 9.

Chapter 9

Quiet Influence Strength #6: Thoughtful Use of Social Media

"In social media what matters are . . . real relationships. Networking is always important when it's real and it's always a useless distraction when it's fake."

Seth Godin, Author and Entrepreneur

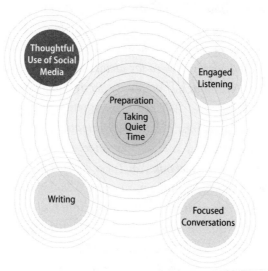

Selah Abrams is a low-key thirty-something engineer at a top global media company. There, Selah has been involved in the operation of several of the organization's most successful social networking initiatives. Additionally, he drove the creation of *a well-respected in-house business resource group for younger employees.*

Selah is also very proud of planting the seeds for the Atlanta chapter of the New Leaders Council (NLC) "which works to train and support the progressive political entrepreneurs of tomorrow—trendsetters, elected officials, and civically engaged leaders in business and industry who will shape the landscape."[44]

His involvement dates back to 2009, when he learned about NLC from a colleague while in Baltimore. Intrigued, he looked up the organization and saw it had a function going on at that very moment in nearby DC. Selah was able to catch the tail end of the meeting. He was won over by the sincerity, effectiveness, focused mission, and friendly environment set by its leaders. Selah reminisces, "From there, it was a no brainer to start up a chapter in Atlanta, where I saw a dire need for the training of the vanguard of young civic and political leadership, regardless of their issue." His efforts, along with the energy of others, paid off. The Atlanta chapter has graduated four classes of civic leaders and was awarded the Digerati Award for social media in 2011.

Selah believes that the chapter's effective use of social media has fueled its success. "When we first starting reaching out to people to gauge interest in a new organization, we got nothing," he said. "By setting up info sessions, meet-ups, and pushing the word out through Facebook, YouTube, Twitter, and LinkedIn, we were able to quickly find the most active and impactful young leaders in our community and establish and build relationships with them." His team also reached out to other organizations and met with "influencers" who they compelled to get on board. Those community leaders tapped into their social networks too, and the chapter grew to national prominence. One alum, Stacey Chavis, praises the chapter for providing "unique training that has empowered me to take my talents to the next level." Not only has she moved into the role of political /public affairs committee chair of the Junior League of Atlanta, she also runs her own company training political leaders and has been named one of Atlanta's 100 Top Black Women of Power. Through leading the chapter's social media efforts, Selah has truly made a difference in Stacey's life and, by extension, the lives that she touches.

In his own quietly thoughtful manner, Selah excels as an innovator and change agent by figuring out who to target and then choosing the right tools to accomplish his goals. As part of the complete growth strategy Selah oversaw, social media gave the Atlanta chapter of NLC a platform with the broadest reach possible. Through this platform, Selah has had a deep and lasting influence on many people.

What do I mean by social media? I am talking about web-based and mobile-based technologies that are used to turn communication into interactive dialogue among organizations, communities, and individuals. Social media gives today's Quiet Influencers a particularly effective and efficient option. These technologies promise to become increasingly potent forces in the future as electronic tools become more refined and widely used. They allow introverts like Selah to organize their thoughts at their own speed and be selective about where and when they place them. They also give those who hesitate to speak in public the opportunity to communicate and collaborate with hundreds or even thousands of people all over the world. For that reason, it may be just the perfect lever for Quiet Influencers now and into the future.

Have you also wondered how you can use social media to get your message across and get others to move forward? When you take the time to engage in purposeful discussion through social media, you can significantly expand your network, provoke new ways of thinking, and challenge the status quo. You can excel at Thoughtful Use of Social Media because you've invested in Taking Quiet Time, taken needed Preparation time, and drawn on your Writing strength. Once you are engaged in social media, you can use it as a way to "listen" online and enter virtual Focused Conversations. In many ways, a Thoughtful Use of Social Media is the Quiet Influence strength of the future. It gives a new form to the traditional strengths of Engaged Listening, Focused Conversations, and Writing.

Are you intrigued but also somewhat anxious about how you can take the plunge into the virtual world? Or are you simply wondering about converting your existing social media activities into an influencing strength? Read on. This chapter will give you tips to use social media in extending the reach of your influence beyond your current circle.

Thoughtful Use of Social Media and Influence

A thoughtful approach to social media helps to raise your QIQ in four key ways. Use it to move people to action, develop and grow relationships, achieve visibility, and teach and learn.

1. Move People to Action

Social movements now rely on social media to mobilize people. Sometimes, this mobilization can lead to historic change. An introverted Google computer engineer named Wael Ghonim has been called a "reluctant revolutionary." He is thought to have sparked 2011's "Arab spring" when he started an anonymous Facebook page that became a focal point for Egyptians and others who took to the streets to change their very societies. In one post he wrote, "The revolution is not going to die or go away. Egyptians will never put up with another pharaoh. Thought is stronger than bullets; ideas never die."[45] Certainly, he was a Quiet Influencer: *Time magazine named him one of the 100 most influential people of 2011.*[46]

Dr. Lisa Rossbacher is another introverted leader on a mission, albeit a less well-known one. As a trained geologist and president of Southern Polytechnic State University in Marietta, Georgia, she is passionate about encouraging more women to enter science, technology, engineering, and math fields (known as STEM). One way she has focused her energies on this issue was to start a blog on the home page of the campus website. Through this vehicle, she advocates her positions. In one post she discussed "the stereotypes that the public has about women in science and technology, stereotypes women have about themselves, and stereotypes that everyone has about the nature of work in technical fields."[47] Lisa uses her blog as a tool of influence to reach many who might not otherwise hear her message. This vehicle has the exponential potential to reach countless girls, women, alumni, employers, and other members of the community.

2. Develop and Grow Relationships

Making a difference in the world starts, quite simply, with building relationships. A thoughtful approach to using social media as part of developing and growing your people connections can greatly improve your influence. Christie Ann Barakat, an assistant professor of social media, says that social media can "supplement and enrich real-life relationships by enabling people to keep in touch, make plans, share. . . . We establish relationships based on shared interests rather than proximity."[48] Effective Quiet Influencers often combine social media and face-to-face relationship-building techniques. They use social media to set the stage for offline meetings or phone calls. Justyn Howard, CEO of Sprout Social, Inc., commented, "Social media has led to many face-to-face meetings I wouldn't have set up otherwise with new colleagues, new friends, and new business partners."[49]

Influence isn't, however, about the quantity of relationships. Introverts, including Quiet Influencers, prefer a few deep relationships to many surface-level ones. Their use of social media mirrors this more focused approach. For instance, they don't seem to be concerned about the number of contacts or "friends" in their social networks. As Seth Godin proposed in the opening quote of this chapter, what's important is the quality of those relationships. Are they ones of meaning where there is a give and take, or are they fake?

Quiet Influencers use social media to strategically build the right relationships in the right way. According to sales and social media expert Barbara Giamanco, co-author of *The New Handshake: Where Sales Meets Social Media,* connecting online makes a difference. The greatest influencers come to social media as "givers" not "takers." The givers, she explains, "think about what they have to offer to people without expecting something in return. They share business referrals, promote colleagues, and recommend resources and ideas." The "takers" use social media "as a megaphone to broadcast sales spam,"[50] says Barbara. That's not effective influence: people see through that approach and quickly lose interest in those "taker" messages. Because Quiet Influencers tend to "give" through other strengths as well (particularly through Engaged Listening, Focused Conversations, and Writing), this advice about success in social media resonates with their general approach to building relationships.

There is a small catch concerning the give-and-take balance. Deanna Zandt, author of *Share This: How You Will Change the World with Social Networking,* writes that you need to share something of yourself in order to be authentic and build connected relationships: "The point of sharing who you are is not to aspire to reality-TV levels of exposure. It's to immerse yourself—or the part of yourself that you feel comfortable sharing—in a conversation that's important and relevant to your life."[51] Ryan Jenkins, the sales professional and speaker on Millenials from chapter 8, recommends that managers reveal more of themselves through social media than they may have in traditional settings in the past. Both the introverts and extroverts in his generation, Ryan explains, have a lower privacy threshold than that of previous generations. He strongly believes his peers are more engaged if their leaders show a slice of themselves on sites such as Facebook and Twitter.

3. Achieve Visibility

For introverts, having an online presence is often a comfortable way of revealing themselves to a much larger community. Others can learn about their unique point of view and gain glimpses into their personality. This self-controlled "exposure" creates a strong, unique presence and makes them more credible influencers in their communities. It raises their profile and gives others an avenue to engage with them and their ideas. The result: these Quiet Influencers are able to provoke new ways of thinking and encourage others to move forward.

Sometimes, even humor can be an excellent way to heighten the visibility of a person or organization. Derrick, a senior editor at a publishing company, posts witty sayings and unusual videos that show a different side of his more taciturn nature. He also writes an organizational e-newsletter that is notorious for its humor and low-key promotion of authors. Readers reveal that they look forward to receiving his monthly transmission because they love being surprised and know they will always collect cool ideas and tips.

Social media can also increase your exposure as a thought leader. According to strategy consultant Dorie Clark, a thought leader is someone who "builds a reputation as a singular expert— someone who doesn't just participate in the conversation, but drives it." She says that it's all about "leverage." "No matter how brilliant and talented you are, you won't be sufficiently appreciated within your organization or by your customers until the broader public recognizes you."[52] In other words, having great ideas doesn't make you influential. You become influential only when you make those ideas visible and accessible to others. It is in that sharing, which is made more efficient and interactive with social media, that thought leaders become influencers who effect change on a broader scale.

4. Teach and Learn

Freely sharing information on social media sites like YouTube is also a powerful way to influence others. Whether explaining how to install memory on a specific computer or teaching a language on iTunes, introverts who might shy away from teaching in front of a classroom now have a comfortable venue to share their skills. These Internet-based outlets provide Quiet Influencers with endless possibilities to make a difference in others' lives. Salman Khan is one Quiet Influencer who has tapped into the teaching power of online video. In 2008, he founded the online Khan Academy (see box). His highly successful website, which is funded by Bill Gates, among others, consists of 3,100 tutoring-type instructional videos. "We're a not-for-profit with the goal of changing education for the better by providing a free world-class education to anyone anywhere," Khan says.[53]

Of course, the other benefit to you as a teacher is your own continuous learning. In addition to producing original content, Quiet Influencers, including those who are thought leaders, also use the pertinent postings, articles, and research discussions found on social media as a way to stay ahead of the curve. They comment on issues, follow people who interest them, and distribute relevant content to their communities. This solid and ever-increasing knowledge base gives them a stronger platform from which to inspire others and provoke new ways of thinking. Quiet Influencers who participate in social media as continuous learners become known as the "go-to" people because of their deep and up-to-date knowledge and ethos.

How to Use Social Media for Influence

Introverted influencers who use social media effectively freely admit they don't have all the answers about how to be most effective in what is still essentially "the wild west" of sites and apps that launch or change each day. To best cut through the noise, they use

---

YES, YOU KHAN

Salman Khan began teaching the world when he made videos to help his young cousin with algebra. He jokes that "she preferred me on YouTube to in person." This experience spurred him to develop more instructional videos, and, in 2008, he founded Khan Academy with the mission to provide a free, world-class education to anyone, anywhere. Since then, more than 158 million videos have been downloaded and the site has seen more than 4.5 million visitors![54] Khan is well on his way to changing education, and ultimately the world, for the better.

Khan Academy's materials and resources, which cover K through 12 math and science topics as well as a few subjects in the humanities, are available to everyone—students and teachers alike—free of charge. The site incorporates social media–proven game mechanics that make learning fun and reward students with badges and points for learning.

One user, a single mother trying to get into nursing school, tweeted about the difference the Khan Academy had made in her life: "I hadn't taken biology, chemistry, or math for a number of years and had forgotten much of what I had learned before. I have gotten A's in all my science courses thanks to your videos! You have saved me in chemistry! Thank you! I know I could never have done this without your wonderful organization. I am on my way to taking care of my children, and I know you will help them as well on their journey to excellent education."[55]

---

three key approaches to integrate social media into their influencing approach: they think about it, engage, and focus on content.

1. Think about It

Know your purpose   Start by defining your goal. If you don't know where you are going, says the old adage, any road will take you there. "Know what your objective is before you plunge into the social media world," says social media expert Barbara

Giamanco. "Technology is like putting gas in the car. It helps drive the strategy, it is not THE strategy.[56]

Ask yourself what you are trying to accomplish through your social media activities. Are you, like Salman Khan, trying to change the world one click at a time? Do you want to initiate conversations to get feedback about your ideas? Are you trying to spread your message to a large audience? Do you want to attract clients, sell products, or position yourself for a new job? Also consider who you are trying to reach: a few of the right people or a lot of the general public? Once you answer these questions, you will have a better idea of how to channel your online efforts. Take for example social media novice Susan, a sales consultant who wanted to attract more small business owners as clients. At the same time that she joined a local Chamber of Commerce group, she connected with entrepreneur groups online. She also created a blog where she weaved in her key messages, and posted guest post entries on other blogger sites. Through her well-crafted social media plan and execution, Susan became known as an expert and made several key connections that resulted in lucrative contracts for her company.

Decide to start somewhere   Resist the pressure to get overwhelmed; take one step forward. Don't try to "do it all." Instead, pick just the two or three social media outlets that will help you meet your goals, and then do a good job on those sites. Limiting your involvement will help make your commitment more manageable.

You'll have to poke around to determine which sites are right for you. Each has a benefit and a potential downside. Social media expert Gina Carr describes Twitter as a cocktail party with little deep conversation but where you can get to know many people in addition to listening and learning. Facebook, on the other hand, is like a backyard barbecue: more informal and useful for connecting in groups.[57]

Note that with few exceptions introverts don't post as much or as frequently as extroverts on Facebook. It feels too intrusive to them and does not allow for enough in-depth conversation. One introvert said, "Facebook isn't intended for introverts like me. I have only a few strong social bonds. In superficial dialogues, like those about a hip new restaurant or a celebrity's faux pas, I prefer not to speak."

LinkedIn tends to be most useful as a serious business tool for sales, job seeking, and front-end research. Selah Abrams wrote, "I LOVE LinkedIn!! It's the social media platform with the least spam and detritus, best focus, awesome search capabilities, and the networks are second to none."

Be aware of emerging trends. In the fast-moving world of social media, your posting options change frequently. What emerging platforms and apps might help you to connect with people and get your message across? Is video still hot? Are mobile applications where it's at? Do a Google search on some of the experts mentioned in this chapter, and you will find up-to-date guidance on social media.

2. Engage

Dedicate ten minutes per day   By limiting the number of social media outlets you use, you will achieve a great deal even if you engage for only ten minutes each day. It's a matter of doing a little of the right activity on a very regular basis.

One of the most time-efficient and powerful social media strategies is to share articles, links, and thoughtful comments on blogs and media sites. By participating in a stream of intriguing back-and-forth dialogues, you become the "giver" mentioned earlier instead of just a "taker." Such online interactions typically occur on more controversial pieces. When you get involved, you may be able to significantly change the conversation on the topic in question. Concentrating on blogs also keeps you abreast of the changing trends in your field so that you can be a more knowledgeable influencer.

Set the stage for deeper relationships   Use social media to set the stage for offline conversations, and then capitalize on the one-on-one opportunities you generate. On LinkedIn, Selah Abrams, explains, "People don't mind being 'cold called' from around the world. They may even give their contact number so we can have an actual old-school phone conversation and get to know each other."

You can also build relationships that ultimately contribute to your professional influence through non–work related social media activities. Music sharing sites for instance allow you to share music playlists and bond with people through a common love of music genres. Virtual games help connect you with acquaintances that you may or may not choose to engage with in other ways.

Find a social media tutor   Quiet Influencers who are uncomfortable taking on social media often buddy up with a knowledgeable friend or colleague or even a teenager who can walk them through some of the basic ins and outs and encourage them along the way. Vicki Austin, a career coach says, "I have what I call 'The Joy Factor'—that is, my friend Joy, who tutors me on social media. She's about ten years younger than I am, an avid Apple user, and a prolific social media communicator. Joy taught me the joys of social media and patiently walked me through the process of applying social media to my business and my life. Some of us need that handholding to overcome our fear or resistance to something we don't yet understand."

3. Focus on Content

Write   Get your thoughts out of your head and onto the screen. Posting your own pieces on social media sites and starting a blog can be real plusses for an introvert who naturally prefers writing to talking. Through the writing process, you can flesh out ideas before you choose to share them with a larger community. "Create useful and timely content and invite others to share it," says

Mike Wittenstein, an introverted customer experience consultant. He invested in learning and maximizing social media to grow his business. Mike reaped the results by signing several major clients who discovered him online. He shared that for him writing is the essence of social media involvement. "Do whatever it takes to get words on paper; any excuse, is, well, just an excuse."

Listen and learn Focus not just on content you create, but on content created by others. Drop in on discussions and visit groups related to your areas of interest. Use the social media universe as a way to conduct research that contributes to your influencing strategies. Increasingly, introverts are using Twitter, for example, as a vehicle to learn. They people watch, virtually. For them, such sites are not about posting as much as they are for reviewing the streams of information from others. The knowledge they pick up about trends and key players often proves invaluable in crafting their influencing strategy. Journalists like Dan Balz, a chief correspondent for the *Washington Post* who covers politics, wrote that four years ago he didn't use social media but now relies on it for most of his leads.

Zev, an introverted nonprofit director, prepares for important conversations and challenging tasks by doing a search on the topic. Before leading his maintenance staff to assemble a pop-up garage kit that had been donated without instructions, he watched several YouTube videos to find out what approaches had worked for others.

When you regularly use content found on social media, you become more aware of what works and what doesn't, and this knowledge will help you improve the content you put out there. You will get used to the appropriate length, tone, pacing, and format, and become a better editor of your own material.

Control your online reputation. Be proactive in keeping your information current and relevant. It is now standard for people to do a search for you online before a first-time meeting or phone call. Finding a link to your high-school track meet scores from

USING SOCIAL MEDIA TO
BECOME A THOUGHT LEADER

Quiet Influencer and consultant Mike Wittenstein often mentors other consultants in building their businesses through social media. Central to the strategy he recommends: position yourself as a thought leader. Mike recommends these four tips to produce content that puts you in the driver's seat of the conversations related to your topic.

1. **Include questions such as "Have you ever asked what makes a great consultant?"** Then go on to write, "I have and here's what I think." Embed the question that you think people who might need your services would ask. That way, your posting will come up in search results including that pertinent question.

2. **Write regularly about what you know.** Be authentic and authoritative. Strive to write one hundred short pieces of quality content (250 to 500 words is usually enough to develop a point of view and make it interesting). Start a folder on your computer called "Blog" and stash ideas in there to access when you have writing time.

3. **Link your writing to what's going on in the world and create and deliver a press release.** Whether you make it into print or not, your release and, possibly, your article or blog post, will live on in multiple locations. Multiple references to the same piece help your content rise to the top of search results when people who don't (yet) know you search for what you know about.

4. **Develop some good Twitter buddies and provide them with draft tweets about your content from their point of view.** It will be really easy for them to help you spread your message. And don't forget to tweet about their work too.

ten years ago is probably not the first thing you want them to find. Have them land first on information you have created. By entering your name into a search tool, you can see what information is now appearing online about you. As mentioned earlier, commenting on other social media sites links your ideas to those of other thought leaders. It also allows you to have more control over your visibility and presence, involving you in a broader conversation and network.

Overuse of Social Media

Quiet Influencers who use social media almost always combine it with other influencing strengths. Because introverts may get sucked into social media, they may run the risk of neglecting other approaches. The secret of a successful social media strategy is moderation. When you overuse it at the expense of other strengths, you may limit your opportunity to influence others. Specifically, overuse takes the form of information overload, ignored audiences, device addiction, and "one-way by the wayside."

1. Information Overload

According to Andrew Weil, MD, information overload is "inimical to focused attention." Social media can feel like a neverending river of information. Because there is no end in sight, it is hard to limit your time and create a workable schedule. If you don't, you will get stressed out before you've found the nuggets you need to formulate your influencing plan.

You can also overload others. Once you get familiar with social media, it becomes easy to post a quick idea or suggestion. Sometimes, that ends up being too many suggestions or opinions. The sea of information is confusing to your followers. Instead of picking a course of action your readers simply shut down and do nothing, and you have missed your opportunity to influence.

Your community is especially likely to resist action when the online postings are so short and succinct that they offer little explanation. When you create a flood of electronic sound bites, you miss the chance to take others on roads of more discovery. Also bear in mind that sharing too much, particularly in the form of unimportant personal updates, can create a negative reputation. People will either dismiss all that you write or go as far as severing the online relationship.

2. Ignored Audiences

A large percentage of the world—many, many introverts among them—either uses social media minimally or not at all. Some people actually take pride in not following the crowd and never engaging on social media. They hang on to their old phones and have a bare-bones virtual footprint that barely registers when their names are searched for online. If you rely on social media as your only or main medium of communication, you will lose key opportunities to learn about these individuals, and even more importantly, to reach them. Because they are not plugged in to social media, you likewise will not be plugged into their concerns, needs, and networks.

3. Device Addiction

Social media does allow you to develop relationships with people who you may not otherwise connect. An "addiction" to social media, however, can strain relationships with those physically near you. If you commonly refresh your tweets while someone is talking to you, you are not able to really listen to that person and you will be perceived as either tuned out or rude. Additionally, when you are on your computer or smartphone, you miss the revealing nuances of someone's voice or body language. You likely will jeopardize in-person relationships as you try to build online ones.

Author and writing instructor Jessica Handler finds it especially annoying to have to compete with the numerous devices in the hands of her writing students. Those who do influence her positively (and receive better grades) are the ones who unplug for the duration of the class. They "show up." "In-person communication," Jessica says, "is still what is going to make you stand out from the crowd."

4. One-Way by the Wayside

Gone are the days of one-way lectures. Online conversations also should be robust enough to spark others to action. People want to have a voice through comments, questions, and critiques on popular sites. If you use social media to pontificate but don't take the time to let your audience question you, ask for clarification, or even disagree strongly with your ideas, you are likely going to lose their listening ear. Steve Spangler, the YouTube Science Guy, welcomes comments.[58] Through contrary opinions and by being open to critiques he learns which topics he should be addressing. Remember that the name of the game is engagement and interactivity. Relying on social media as a platform to present one-way communication simply does not work.

Your Next Steps

Social media is a perfect fit for Quiet Influencers. It opens up unprecedented avenues for influencing a broader community than was ever possible before the widespread adoption of the Internet. Learn how to use social media effectively and in moderation. If you do so, it can become the influencing strength that makes the biggest difference in your ability to make a wide reaching difference.

To increase your ability to use social media for influence, begin by reviewing the key points from this chapter:

1. The greatest social media influencers are "givers" not "takers."

2. Use social media to create visibility for your cause or ideas.

3. Remember that content is king. Concentrate on posting high-quality, thought-provoking material.

4. Focus on just a few sites that resonate with you rather than spreading yourself too thin.

5. Encourage and solicit contrary opinions when sharing ideas on social media.

Once you have a handle on those basics, apply them to your own situation through these questions:

1. What new knowledge or connections have you gained from social media sites? How was this knowledge presented, and what can you learn from the techniques used?

2. How do you prioritize where to spend your time on social media? What resources are you drawing upon for content to post?

3. How can you use social media as a tool to gather research for your current influencing challenge? How can you use the technology to disseminate your ideas?

Congratulations! With an understanding of Thoughtful Use of Social Media, you now have reviewed the full portfolio of Quiet Influencing strengths. The next chapter will walk you through what to do next in order to make a difference.

Chapter 10

Making a Quiet Difference

"Do not underestimate the determination of a quiet man."

Iain Duncan Smith, British Politician

As I write this conclusion, I am reflecting on a series of group coaching calls I had today with Quiet Influencers in an information technology organization. As we discussed some of their leadership hurdles, I couldn't help but notice the obvious preparation they had done for the call. Every now and then, the line was silent as they carefully thought about their words and shared their insights and experience to help others on the call move forward. To me, these productive sessions presented a microcosm of Quiet Influence at its best.

Like these professionals who aspire to make a difference, the people you met in this book and the experience and lessons they shared imparted a key message: introverts can be highly effective influencers when they make the most of their own natural strengths instead of trying to act like extroverts.

I believe their stories have staying power. I hope you remember Julie and how Taking Quiet Time helped her hatch a lifesaving initiative. I trust that you'll be inspired by the story of Jake's perseverance and how his intensive use of Preparation paid off for a tough teacher training initiative. When you need to tune into a person, perhaps you will recall how Elisha's Engaged Listening made such a powerful difference in building trust. And as you plan a new initiative, you may remember Haley Kilpatrick's effective use of Focused Conversations as she launched Girl Talk and helped so many young girls grow in self-confidence. When you face an opportunity to persuade others through Writing, you can think of Helen Thorpe and how her compassionate writing helped readers understand the backstory of immigration. And humble Selah Abrams may come to mind when you want to bring about change by tapping into the power of a Thoughtful Use of Social Media to rock the world.

Each of these Quiet Influencers and the many others profiled in this book went beyond their comfort zones to talk about themselves and their strengths. My greatest hope is that you will be inspired by their stories to reach into your own rich reservoir of strengths to stretch to new levels of influence.

From Inspiration to Action

Move from inspiration to action by putting your own influencing plans in place. Take the next step by reflecting on these questions and record your answers.

1. Which stories from the book particularly inspired you? What lessons did they demonstrate?

2. Now that you've read the book, review your QIQ results in chapter 3. What strength is the highest priority for you to focus on now?

3. Take a look at the five summary points in "Your Next Steps" at the end of chapters 4 through 9. Which two or three tools or tips resonated the most with you in each chapter?

4. Look at your responses to the questions at the end of chapters 4 through 9. How can you use your newfound

insights to address the influencing challenge you identified at the end of chapter 3?

Now it's time to move beyond reflection and into doing something about that influencing challenge. Consider these steps:

1. Sketch out a brief influencing plan or develop a more elaborate one to address your influencing challenge.

2. Sit with it for a few days.

3. Run it by someone you trust and then adapt it as you see fit.

4. Take action and reward yourself for moving forward on your Quiet Influencing journey!

"Poco a Poco"

No matter where you start, always remember to acknowledge your efforts in trying on new influencing behaviors. Savor each moment of success and learn from things that don't go exactly as planned. As the Spanish expression goes, it's "poco a poco"—or in English, "little by little." Don't get overwhelmed and think you have to try all the new ideas in this book at once. Persevere along your journey one step at a time instead of trying to make a wholesale change right away. Remember, influencing is a process, not an event. You will fail and you will succeed. Both experiences will move you forward and increase your QIQ. Progress comes from being willing to try and stay open to continuous learning.

And your reward? Seeing that you are successfully challenging ingrained ways of thinking, that your new ideas are taking hold, that changes you envisioned are coming about, and that others are moving forward with your inspiration. In your own quiet way, you will be making the difference that you were naturally born to make.

Your Quiet Influence Quotient (QIQ) Self-Assessment Product

To help you assess your Quiet Influence Quotient (QIQ) and create an individual action plan, we've created a self-assessment to test your strengths and improvement opportunities. This online companion includes an interpretation of your score and suggested next steps. It will provide you with a way to assess your progress as you apply the ideas in the book.

You may also print your results, forward them to others, and ask others to take the test to gain additional feedback on how they view your QIQ. This unique online companion product is available at *www.bkconnection.com/quiet-influence-sa*.

Bulk-order discounts are available for teams,
book clubs, and organizations.

Notes

Introduction

1. Jay Conger, "The Necessary Art of Persuasion," *Harvard Business Review*, May–June 1998, 85–95.

Chapter 1

2. Jennifer B. Kahnweiler, PhD, online survey, June 2009.
3. Susan Cain, *Quiet: The Power of Introverts in a World that Can't Stop Talking* (New York: Crown, 2012) 4.

Chapter 2

4. Richard Stengel, managing editor, *Time* magazine, April 30, 2012, 6.
5. Adam Lashinsky, "How Tim Cook Is Changing Apple," *Fortune*, May 24, 2013, 110–118.

Chapter 4

6. Susan Cain, *Quiet: The Power of Introverts in a World that Can't Stop Talking* (New York: Crown, 2012) 82–83.
7. Sharon Begley, "The Science of Making Decisions," www.thedailybeast.com/newsweek/2011/02/27/i-can-t-think.html, February 27, 2011.
8. James Thayer, *Author: A Publication of the Northwest Writers Association*, www.authormagazine.org/articles/thayer_james_2009_04_09.htm, February 27, 2011.

9. Sophia Dembling, *The Introvert's Way: Living A Quiet Life in a Noisy World* (New York: Penguin, 2012).

10. Eric van Heck, "New Way of Working: Microsoft's Mobility Office," *RSM Insight,* First Quarter 2010, 5.

Chapter 5

11. Jay A. Fernandez, "*Hunger Games* producer Nina Jacobson on Movie Back-Story; Firing from Disney" (Q&A), by *The Hollywood Reporter,* March 15, 2012.

12. Jennifer B. Kahnweiler, PhD, survey of one hundred introverts, June 2009.

13. Douglas Conant, "Are You an Introverted Boss?" *Harvard Business Review,* April 4, 2011.

14. Robert Weide (director), *Woody Allen: A Documentary.* American Masterpiece. July 21, 2011.

15. Al Pittampelli on the Modern Meeting, AMA Edgewise Podcast, September 2, 2011.

16. Basarab, Dave, *Predictive Evaluation: Ensuring Training Delivers Business and Organizational Results* (San Francisco: Berrett-Koehler, 2011).

17. David Greenberg, personal communication, January 2010.

18. Barbara McAfee, *Full Voice: The Art and Practice of Vocal Presence* (San Francisco: Berrett-Koehler, 2011).

19. Jennifer B. Kahnweiler, PhD, *The Introverted Leader: Building on Your Quiet Strength* (San Francisco: Berrett-Koehler, 2009), 19–24.

Chapter 6

20. Adam M. Grant, Francesca Gino, and David A. Hofmann, "Reversing the Extraverted Leadership Advantage: The Role of Employee Proactivity," *The Academy of Management Journal,* Vol. 54, No. 3 (2011), 528–550.

21. Stewart Levine, *Getting to Resolution: Turning Conflict to Collaboration,* 2nd ed. (San Francisco: Berrett-Koehler, 2009).

22. www.thedailybeast.com/newsweek/2012/05/06/melinda-gates-new-crusade-investing-billions-in-women-s-health.html.

23. Oprah Winfrey's Master Class radio interview with Morgan Freeman, OWN, aired June 17, 2012.

24. Walter Mossberg, "The Steve Jobs I Knew," *Wall Street Journal*, October 5, 2011.

25. Adam Bryant, "Xerox's New Chief Tries to Defend its Culture," *New York Times*, February 10, 2010.

26. Barbara McAfee, *Full Voice: The Art and Practice of Vocal Presence* (San Francisco: Berrett-Koehler, 2011) 5–6.

Chapter 7

27. Haley Kilpatrick with Whitney Joiner, *The Drama Years: Real Girls Talk about Surviving Middle School—Bullies, Brands, Body Image, and More* (New York: Free Press, 2012).

28. Doug Conant, *Touch Points: Creating Powerful Leadership Connections in the Smallest of Moments* (San Francisco: Jossey-Bass, 2011). See also http://conantleadership.com.

29. Cliff Kuang, "The Brainstorming Process Is B.S. but Can We Rework It?" *Fast Company*, www.fastcodesign.com/1668930/the-brainstorming-process-is-bs-but-can-we-rework-it, January 2012.

30. "Quiet Strength," *Pulse Magazine*, http://blogs.ajc.com/atlanta-job-blog/2009/08/25/pulse-quiet-strength

31. Linda Tischer, Fast Company, www.fastcompany.com/1826824/how-john-maeda-sold-risds-faculty-his-vision-school, April 16, 2012.

32. Sam Horn, "Intriguing Insights on How to Create Compelling Communications that Pass the Eyebrow Test." http://samhornpop.wordpress.com/tag/the-eyebrow-test

Chapter 8

33. Helen Thorpe, *Just Like Us: The True Story of Four Mexican Girls Coming of Age in America* (New York: Scribner, 2011).

34. Helen Thorpe, "The Human Face of Immigration: A Reading and Discussion of *Just Like Us*," ALA Midwinter Conference, 2011.

35. Mark Levy (author of *Accidental Genius*, San Francisco: Berrett-Koehler, 2010), from a news release.

36. Jessica Handler, phone interview, March 18, 2012.

37. Letter from Morgan Stanley, "Why I Am Leaving Goldman Sachs," *New York Times*, March 14, 2012, www.nytimes.com/2012/03/14/opinion/why-i-am-leaving-goldman-sachs.html

38. Tony Alessandra and Michael J. O'Connor, *The Platinum Rule: Discover the Four Basic Business Personalities and How They Can Lead You to Success* (New York, Warner 1996).

39. Blake Gopnik, "The Accidental Art Mogul," *Newsweek*, November 28, 2011, 53.

40. Jessica Handler, phone interview, March 18, 2012.

41. Jessica Handler, phone interview, March 18, 2012.

42. Sunni Brown, Brightspot I.D., "Most Creative Professionals," *Fast Company*, www.fastcompany.com/most-creative-people/2011/sunni-brown-brightspot-id, June 2011.

43. John D. Ramage and John C. Bean, *Writing Arguments*, 4th Ed. (Needham Heights, Mass.: Allyn & Bacon, 1998), 81–82.

Chapter 9

44. The New Leaders Council, http://newleaderscouncil.org/chapters/.

45. Mike Giglio, "Reluctant Revolutionary," *Newsweek*, October 31, 2011, 45.

46. *The 2011 Time 100*, www.time.com/time/specials/packages/article/0,28804,2066367_2066369_2066437,00.html.

47. Lisa Rossbacher, PhD, "Barbie and The Stereotype Threat," the Highered Leadership Blog, http://higheredleadership.wordpress.com/2012/04/05/barbie-and-the-stereotype-threat/, April 5, 2012.

48. Christie Ann Barakat, adjunct professor of media and psychology, Florence University of the Arts, Quora.com site in response to the question "Is Social Media Making Us More Anti-Social?" posted on March 1, 2011.

49. Justyn Howard, CEO Sprout Social, Quora.com site in response to the question "Is Social Media Making Us More Anti-Social?" posted on February 28, 2011.

50. Joan Curtis and Barbara Giamanco, *The New Handshake: Where Sales Meets Social Media* (Santa Barbara, Calif.: Praeger, 2010).

51. Deanna Zandt, *Share This: How You Will Change the World with Social Networking* (San Francisco: Berrett-Koehler, 2010), 93.

52. Dorie Clark, "How to Become a Thought Leader in Six Steps," *HBR Blog Network*, November 9, 2010. http://blogs.hbr.org/cs/2010/11/how_to_become_a_thought_leader.html

53. Salman Khan, Khan Academy Fact Sheet, May 2012, www .khanacademy.com.

54. Salman Khan, Khan Academy Fact Sheet, May 2012, www .khanacademy.com.

55. Salman Khan, Khan Academy Fact Sheet, May 2012, www .khanacademy.com.

56. Barbara Giamanco, personal communication, April 2012.

57. Gina Carr, personal communication, April 2012.

58. National Speakers Association Conference, Certified Speaking Professional Workshop, Indianapolis, Indiana, July 2012.

Acknowledgments

I wrote this book with family, friends, and colleagues, who together have been a bedrock of support.

First, I acknowledge my "Grey Gardens sister" and #1 heroine, my mom, Lucille Boretz. From Willow Road to West 81st Street, your warm, affirming nods, engaged listening, and focused conversations provided a cocoon of love.

Next, I recognize my late loving dad, Alvin Boretz, a brilliant writer who inspired me to make my mark and make a difference. Dad, I learned to embrace my own writing voice by listening to yours. I always felt close to you when tapping into my creative soul.

I am indebted to my husband and best friend of forty plus years, Billy: you fancy yourself a curmudgeon, but we all know better. And because I am giving compliments . . . your delicious dinners have definitely improved with each book.

I deeply appreciate all the ways my children have helped me down this path. Knowing you are living such rich, fulfilling lives freed me up to focus on the work at hand. Jessie, your creative flame lit mine on so many days. You demonstrate perseverance and joy. Lindsey, your grounded feet guided mine steadily to earth. You live balance and compassion. Adam, you are a living example of quiet humility. (It is okay that the CD about networking for introverts is still shrink-wrapped.)

I also acknowledge my sister Carrie Boretz Keating and her family, my Aunt Arline Garson, who defies all aging stereotypes, my late mother-in-law—and dear friend—Ruth Kahnweiler who I miss everyday. Though she once told me I "could get a tree to talk," it was she who was the true champion of rapport. My father-in-law, Louis has always offered generosity, wit, and love.

So many others helped me to make this book a reality. I respected Katherine Armstrong as a colleague before we began our partnership as author and editor many months ago. Since then, I am in awe of the talent, wisdom, and heart she poured into this book. Katherine, I will always be deeply indebted to you for bringing out my best. Arlene Cohn is my right-hand woman. She is a whiz at what she does and has the absolute best giggle this side of the Mississippi.

My Berrett-Koehler publishing family is a team of beautiful Quiet Influencers. I feel infinitely blessed to have landed at your doorstep. I thank my editor, Steve Piersanti, for his vision and humanity. Steve, you were right (most of the time) and pushed me to new important places for which I was grateful afterward. Jeevan Sivasubramaniam, my favorite introvert phone buddy, acted as my patient birth coach in shepherding a rough idea to reality. Overwhelming thanks to marketing wizard and cheerleader Kristen Frantz: I will always love laughing with you over a glass of wine. I'd also like to recognize wunderkinds Katie Sheehan, Johanna Vondeling, Maria Jesus Aguilo, Dianne Platner, David Marshall, Charlotte Ashlock, Rick Wilson, Catherine Legronne, Mike Crowley, Neal Maillot, Marina Cook, Zoe Mackey, and Courtney Schonfeld, who take a book and make it fly. I also am indebted to the reviewers of this manuscript; Roger S. Peterson, Danielle Goodman, Gauri Reyes, and Ed Callaway, and book producer Jonathan Peck of Dovetail Publishing Services who did an exemplary job in shaping the outcome.

Thank you also to the numerous people who generously agreed to share their personal stories about Quiet Influence. Many of their names are listed in the book; others asked to remain anonymous. I am so grateful to all of you who spent from a few minutes to a few hours with me. Let me give a special quiet shout to Selah Abrams, Haley Kilpatrick, Elisha Holtzclaw, Julie Irving, Josh Crafford, Sophia Dembling, Walter May, Jessica Handler, Wally Bock, Vinay Kumar, Jody Wirtz, Barbara Giamanco, Gina Carr, Mike Wittenstein, Michelle Martin, and Ryan Jenkins, and Doug Conant for the extra time and attention they gave to this project.

Thank you to the many others in the wings offering support and invaluable insights. Buckets of gratitude to colleagues, clients and friends Susan Cain, Dan Pink, Adam Grant, David Greenberg, Ken Futch, Gene Greissman, Marty Mercer, Dave Basarab, Darcy Eikenberg, John Kosar, Porter Poole, Ann Jackson, Lisa Rossbacher, Jalaj Garg, Bill Stainton, Brian Walter, Daniel Lee, Ken Blanchard, Jim Kouzes, Mark Levy, Barbara McAfee, Beverly Kaye, Larry Dressler, Jesse Stoner, Kelly Vandever, Lisa Sharp, John Schuster, Ricky Steele, Roosevelt Thomas, Terry Brock, Niki Rabren, Barbara Davis, Diane Samuelson, Sheryl Bruff, Heather Sherbert, Jeannie Fox Craig, Susan Zeidman, Dudley White, Alan Brewer, Ruth Stergiou, Andrea Iadanza, Amy Shaffer, Peggy Collins Freehery, Mindy Nelson, Ellen Green, Vicki Halsey, Chip Bell, Collette Carlson, Gayle Lantz, Devora Zack, Maren Showkeir, Jamie Showkeir, Bill Treasurer, John Schuster, Larry Dressler, Stewart Levine, John Kador, Elizabeth Doty, Roger Stix, Elissa Amerson, Niki Toney-Pressley, Shirley Garrett, Kathleen Dupont, Patti Danos, Tricia Molloy, Helena Brantley, Lisa McLeod, Lloyd Spann, John Courtney, Sandy Heffernan, Lan Bercu, Shari Barth, Laura Goodrich, Perry Pidgeon Hooks, Jennifer Bridges, Rusty Shelton, Andrea Sanchez, Susan Savkov, Shelby Sledge, Nick Alter, Margie Adler, Laura Davis, Amy and

Ken Krupsky, Bobbie Wunch, Ruth and Steve Kleinrock, Charlotte Tucker, Linda Robinson, Heidi Remak Ziff, my Saturday morning women's group, and my NSA and NSA-GA buddies.

There are so many others who have expressed tangible and intangible support, and I hope you know who you are. I will be eternally grateful.

Index

About Jennifer

Photo courtesy of Josh Hobgood

Jennifer Kahnweiler, PhD, is an author, speaker, and executive coach who has been hailed as a "champion for introverts." Her bestselling book *The Introverted Leader: Building on Your Quiet Strength* achieved widespread appeal and has been translated into six languages including Chinese and Spanish.

Her thirty-five-year journey to become an expert on introverts included jobs as an elementary school counselor, university administrator, federal government program director, and career coach. She also deepened her knowledge and appreciation for introverts through her work as a learning and development professional working inside leading organizations such as GE, AT&T, NASA, Turner Broadcasting, and the CDC. Jennifer became committed to championing quieter people, first by helping organizations recognize and value them, and second, by helping introverted individuals step confidently into leadership and influencing roles.

Through keynote speeches and seminars on the topic that include her characteristic humor, poignant stories, and practical tools, she transfers the lessons introverts teach us. Jennifer has also written articles about introverts in the workplace for *Forbes, Bloomberg Business Week*, and the *Wall Street Journal* and has been quoted on the subject in more than fifty international news media outlets, including the *New York Times* and *Time* magazine's January 2012 cover story on introverts.

Jennifer received her Ph.D. in counseling and organizational development at Florida State University and her earlier degrees in sociology and counseling at Washington University, St. Louis. She is a recipient of the 2012 Certified Speaking Professional (CSP) award, the National Speaker's Association's highest earned designation. She has also served on the board of the Berrett-Koehler Author's Co-op and is on the board of the National Speakers Association of Georgia, where she heads up the community service program.

Truth be told, though, the greatest inspiration for her work with introverts has been her forty-year marriage to her husband, Bill. It has been said that couples start to resemble each other after a period of time. Over these four decades, Jennifer has indeed embraced some of Bill's introverted tendencies and developed her own quiet strengths.

She is the grateful mother of three children, Jessie, Lindsey, and Adam. Though she is happy to call Atlanta, Georgia, home, her native New York will always be "the city." She adores yoga (except the hot kind), can turn shopping into an art form, and appreciates any chance to escape to an amazing Korean spa off of I-85. Her most surprising lifetime about-face involves feline friends. She wrote in her high school yearbook that she "hated" cats. And today? She savors quiet time with Fred, the Kahnweiler cat (even though he likes Bill better).

Working with the Author

"Jennifer wowed the group. She has the rare combination of delivering 'news you can use' mixed with humor and authenticity. . . . Both introverts and extroverts alike were buzzing about their insights and next steps long after the meeting ended."

—Heather Rocker, former executive director,
Women in Technology

Jennifer B. Kahnweiler, PhD, CSP, BCC, is an international speaker and executive coach who helps organizations bring out the best in their introverted talent. Programs include engaging keynote speeches, content-rich full-day seminars and shorter webinars, self-directed learning opportunities, and results-driven group and executive coaching.

Keynote Speeches

Quiet Influence: How Introverts Make a Difference

The key message of this session is that you don't have to act like an extrovert to make an impact. In this interactive presentation, Jennifer draws upon important lessons from highly effective Quiet Influencers. Participants learn how to make the most of six natural strengths to challenge the status quo, provoke new ways of thinking, effect change, and inspire others to move forward. They learn a powerful process for raising their Quiet Influence Quotient (QIQ). Both introverts and extroverts gain awareness and knowledge from this powerful presentation.

The Introverted Leader: Building on Your Quiet Strength

In this enlightening and highly engaging program, Jennifer draws upon stories and research from her book of the same name to show how introverts can succeed as leaders and work *with*, not *against*, who they are. Participants learn about the characteristics of introverts, the 4 Ps success strategies of introverted leaders, and why our organizations can't afford to miss out on the invaluable contributions of their quieter employees.

In-House Seminars

Jennifer's highly rated workshops take a deep dive into work challenges by applying key tools and principles of introverted leadership and influence. Two popular seminars are *The Introverted Leader* and *Quiet Influence*, both of which include content from her popular keynote speeches, self-assessments, workbooks, case studies, and role-plays. She also works with organizations to custom design programs using modules that include Networking, Coaching, Focused Conversations, and Thoughtful Use of Social Media.

Webinars

An expert in the use of distant learning technologies, Jennifer offers webinars that range between one and two hours in length. Webinars are an efficient way of delivering program content in a short period of time while reducing travel costs. Both keynotes and seminar topics can be adapted to this format.

Self-Directed Learning Opportunities

Books

Print books or digital editions of the *Quiet Influence: The Introvert's Guide to Making a Difference* and *The Introverted Leader: Building on Your Quiet Strength* can be included with all keynote, seminar, and self-directed learning programs at a significantly reduced cost.

"Learning Bursts"

The *Introverted Leader* program is available through a unique and innovative learning method called the "Learning Burst." Through a unique partnership with consultant and author Dave Basarab, this process gives participants an opportunity to learn without having to disrupt their daily workflow. A Learning Burst is a combination of a ten-minute audiocast and a workbook of supporting material. The workbook contains easy digestible summaries, quizzes, and exercises to apply and cement the learning points. Audio segments are in mp3 format. For more information, visit our website at www.jenniferkahnweiler.com.

PDUs2Go

We also partner with PDUs2Go and provide several *Introverted Leader* courses that help project managers meet their Project Management Institute continuing education requirements. Visit *www.pdus2go.com* to learn more.

Coaching

Group Coaching

Introverted (and extroverted) participants gain great value by discussing provocative questions after seminars and keynotes. Jennifer provides a series of small, extended post-session coaching groups via phone or Skype to give participants an opportunity to engage in focused conversations and problem solving. They share successes, present challenges, and receive peer feedback and clear direction in the safe environment she creates. Group coaching also helps the keynote or seminar's messages "stick" in a lasting and meaningful way.

Executive Coaching

Jennifer B. Kahnweiler, PhD, is a Board Certified Coach with more than twenty-five years of experience providing one-on-one coaching to professionals around the world. She specializes in bringing out the strengths of introverted professionals who want to develop their leadership and influencing skills. Clients appreciate her "velvet hammer" approach, which includes support with accountability.

Contact Information

To learn more, visit *www.jenniferkahnweiler.com* or send an email to *info@jenniferkahnweiler.com*. Become part of her Quiet Influence community by connecting with her on Linked In (Jennifer Kahnweiler), following her on Twitter (JennKahnweiler), and liking her on Facebook (Quiet Influence and The Introverted Leader pages).

Also by Jennifer Kahnweiler

The Introverted Leader
Building on Your Quiet Strength

Being an introvert doesn't mean you can't be a great leader. Citing examples of highly successful leaders like Bill Gates and Warren Buffett, Jennifer Kahnweiler shows that introverts can build on their quiet strength and make it a source of great power. She details a straightforward four-step process to handle work situations such as managing up, leading projects, public speaking, and many more. Kahnweiler provides numerous examples and leadership tips as well as a revealing Introverted Leader Quiz that pinpoints where focused attention will produce maximum results.

"Finally, a book that recognizes the immense value that introverts bring to the workplace."

—Daniel H. Pink, author of *A Whole New Mind*, *Drive*, and *To Sell Is Human*

Paperback, 176 pages, ISBN 978-1-60994-200-7
PDF ebook, ISBN 978-1-57675-587-7

BK® Berrett–Koehler Publishers, Inc.
San Francisco, *www.bkconnection.com*

800.929.2929

Berrett–Koehler
Publishers

Berrett-Koehler is an independent publisher dedicated to an ambitious mission: *Creating a World That Works for All.*

We believe that to truly create a better world, action is needed at all levels—individual, organizational, and societal. At the individual level, our publications help people align their lives with their values and with their aspirations for a better world. At the organizational level, our publications promote progressive leadership and management practices, socially responsible approaches to business, and humane and effective organizations. At the societal level, our publications advance social and economic justice, shared prosperity, sustainability, and new solutions to national and global issues.

A major theme of our publications is "Opening Up New Space." Berrett-Koehler titles challenge conventional thinking, introduce new ideas, and foster positive change. Their common quest is changing the underlying beliefs, mindsets, institutions, and structures that keep generating the same cycles of problems, no matter who our leaders are or what improvement programs we adopt.

We strive to practice what we preach—to operate our publishing company in line with the ideas in our books. At the core of our approach is stewardship, which we define as a deep sense of responsibility to administer the company for the benefit of all of our "stakeholder" groups: authors, customers, employees, investors, service providers, and the communities and environment around us.

We are grateful to the thousands of readers, authors, and other friends of the company who consider themselves to be part of the "BK Community." We hope that you, too, will join us in our mission.

A BK Life Book

This book is part of our BK Life series. BK Life books change people's lives. They help individuals improve their lives in ways that are beneficial for the families, organizations, communities, nations, and world in which they live and work. To find out more, visit **www.bk-life.com**.

Berrett–Koehler
Publishers

A community dedicated to creating
a world that works for all

Visit Our Website: www.bkconnection.com

Read book excerpts, see author videos and Internet movies, read
our authors' blogs, join discussion groups, download book apps, find
out about the BK Affiliate Network, browse subject-area libraries of
books, get special discounts, and more!

Subscribe to Our Free E-Newsletter, the *BK Communiqué*

Be the first to hear about new publications, special discount offers,
exclusive articles, news about bestsellers, and more! Get on the list
for our free e-newsletter by going to **www.bkconnection.com.**

Get Quantity Discounts

Berrett-Koehler books are available at quantity discounts for orders
of ten or more copies. Please call us toll-free at (800) 929-2929 or
email us at bkp.orders@aidcvt.com.

Join the BK Community

BKcommunity.com is a virtual meeting place where people from
around the world can engage with kindred spirits to create a world
that works for all. **BKcommunity.com** members may create their own
profiles, blog, start and participate in forums and discussion groups,
post photos and videos, answer surveys, announce and register for
upcoming events, and chat with others online in real time. Please join
the conversation!

MIX
Paper from
responsible sources

FSC
www.fsc.org   **FSC® C012752**

Certified

Corporation
bcorporation.net